FIRESIDE

Jane Boutelle's LIFETIME FITNESS for Women

Jane Boutelle, B.S., M.A.
Samm Sinclair Baker

F

A FIRESIDE BOOK
PUBLISHED BY SIMON AND SCHUSTER

Copyright © 1978 by Jane Boutelle and Samm Sinclair Baker
All rights reserved
including the right of reproduction
in whole or in part in any form
Published by SIMON and SCHUSTER
A Division of Gulf & Western Corporation
Simon & Schuster Building
Rockefeller Center
1230 Avenue of the Americas
New York, New York 10020

Manufactured in the United States of America

1 2 3 4 5 6 7 8 9 10

Library of Congress Cataloging in Publication Data

Boutelle, Jane.
    Jane Boutelle's Lifetime fitness for women.

    (A Fireside book)
    1. Exercise for women. 2. Physical fitness for
women.   I. Baker, Samm Sinclair, joint author.
II. Title. III. Title: Lifetime fitness for women.
RA781.B69   1978b   613.7 045   78-26547
ISBN 0-671-22937-0
ISBN 0-671-24856-1 Pbk.

Dedicated with love
to the Godmother and Godfather
of this book—
Nancy and Jim Smith

Contents

Jane Boutelle's
LIFETIME FITNESS
for Women

I

Why This Lifetime Fitness Method Succeeds Where Others Fail

At last . . . this book will help you attain the beautifying, energizing, all-over fitness you want, no matter how many times you may have failed before. You will learn exactly *how* in clear, simple, proved ways never told before. *You will see and feel thrilling improvement in your figure and grace within one week!* You will firm off flabby inches joyously. And you will have this life-improving guide on hand for all your healthier years ahead.

What makes all this possible now? First, realize happily that this is not a tiresome "exercise" program, but a different, *enjoyable* method unlike anything you have ever known. From now on, old-fashioned, straining, UNnatural "ex-er-cises" are *out* for you—no more forcing your body into UNnatural, harmful contortions.

Instead, you will be conditioned smoothly both *outside-in* and *inside-out* through flowing-motion Boutelle *natural-actions*. You will become "alignment- and posture-perfect," the basis of bodily health, beauty and grace in every move you make. You will learn "rhythmic-flow breathing" and new "rhythmic pacing" that lead to maximum energy and endurance. "It's such fun!" my students say— no dumbbells, no apparatus, no weights, no slantboards, no gadgets

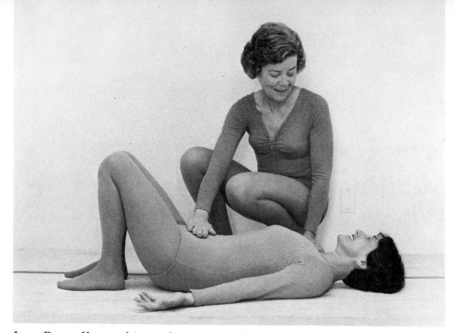

Jane Boutelle teaching a basic natural-action.

or gimmicks—just pleasurable natural-actions with your own body as your best equipment.

You can be sure you will succeed because the Boutelle Method, never before available outside my classes, has worked wonders for the thousands I have taught in over twenty years as a movement specialist. I designed this program for the marvelous uniqueness of you as a woman. Starting now, you can look, feel and function at your top personal capacity at every age—that's *lifetime fitness through natural-actions.*

YOURS: "THAT BEAUTIFUL BOUTELLE LOOK"

You will develop as a natural part of your bearing what a student described as "that beautiful Boutelle look." It is the look of your firmed, deeply conditioned body held proudly and easily in correct alignment, posture-perfect when standing, sitting, moving. Your head is confidently high and poised, your movements smooth, graceful, seemingly effortless—without self-consciousness or strain. "That beautiful Boutelle look" radiates all-over fitness and magnetic vitality, attracting outspoken admiration.

Note just a few of the all-important differences and superiorities (details later) of your Boutelle program:

1. Natural-actions are designed for *female* (not male) body structure, to condition a woman's muscles, organs, and systems in harmony with her natural functioning—*no forcing, straining, UNnatural manipulations.* (As you move smoothly, enjoying your body's rhythmic functioning, it becomes obvious why so many women have hated "exercise" and calisthenics created basically for the *male* body.)

2. You will see quick results. As you learn almost immediately how to "think IN" and "think UP," standing TALL and pulling your abdominal muscles IN, you will look as though you have *lost about five pounds* around your middle. And a tape measure test will prove that your waistline is *up to two inches smaller* with ideal Boutelle posture.

3. You will learn how to become *alignment-aware.* No other method has ever emphasized and taught correct body alignment as you will learn it here. Any knowledgeable physician or anatomy expert knows that you cannot function best unless your body is correctly aligned—yet most bodies are *out of alignment* (watch the slumping, unattractive way most people walk, stand, sit). Just standing and sitting with feet and knees tight together, as taught by many so-called fitness specialists, throws the body badly out of alignment. Your Boutelle program can correct that at any age, and helps overcome past undesirable practices leading to back problems and other painful injuries.

4. You will achieve not just "physical fitness," but new *neuromuscular fitness,* bringing muscular and nervous systems into harmony, helping to relieve stress and release tension. It is the buildup of stress *without the release of tension* that often leads to serious trouble. (The dictionary defines neuromuscular as "affecting both *nerves* and *muscles.*")

5. Most concepts of "exercise" are *external,* but Boutelle natural-actions condition you *inside-out* as well as outside-in, moving all 632 muscles, all joints. They work deep in your digestive, respiratory, and circulatory systems, as other programs and sports do not (even swimming, an excellent activity, does not work deep in your digestive tract, and should be supplemented by natural-actions). Total inside-out conditioning prepares the body to withstand problems and come back quickly from pregnancy, surgery, illnesses, physical and emotional problems.

6. With brief, enjoyable daily sessions, you progress from the starting "A" Alpha program to the advanced "B" Best program. Your body builds energy and endurance, and you function at the very best you can be for your physiological and chronological age. You look beautifully graceful as you learn to maintain your correct body alignment and posture. You prevent many difficulties from demanding sports and recreational activities, and from aging, by keeping your body tuned-up, free-moving, with good muscle tone and flexibility.

REVEALING CASE HISTORIES

Arlene W., age 34: Before she started the Boutelle program, she was flabby and complained, "I always feel pooped." A short time later she told me, "I'm not only full of vim and vigor, but *I've dropped two dress sizes.* And your tape measure test shows that *I've taken inches off* my waist, hips and thighs." Her figure is unbelievably trim and buoyant.

Susan B., 42: She came in out of condition, out of alignment, and kinked over by a bad back. She sighed, "I've had to give up sports. I don't think I'll ever move gracefully again." After a year, she sent me a postcard: "I've been playing tennis every day here in Bermuda with my husband. I have a new lease on life, and I thank you for it."

Beverly C., 28: Pale and dispirited, moving like a stick, Bev joined my Medical Referral program (Chapter IX) after a mastectomy, at her doctor's insistence. As she learned correct alignment and posture, and began using her body smoothly and effortlessly with the help of natural-actions, she soon carried herself proudly. I treasure a hastily scrawled note from her: "When you first met me, I was depressed and doubted my femininity. Now I run and dance and play better than I ever did before. Bless you, Jane."

Kim P., 38: A beautiful, spirited woman, she is a member of one of my favorite families. Her mother, Diana, 59, a Boutelle participant for years, is a top golfer, with one of the best figures I've seen at any age. Kim loves my classes so much that she brought her daughter, Pamela, a delightful teenager. Soon Pam told me, "When

I have a little girl, I want advance enrollment for her." That will make four generations of the family in the Boutelle program!

Lenore T., 63: After a truck slid into her car on a snowy road, she wrote to me from the hospital: "I've bounced back so fast from my operation that my doctor and nurses are amazed. They agree with me that it's due to my fine 'neuromuscular' condition, thanks to your program, Jane. I'll be back in top form soon after I get out of here." Incidentally, her daughter, Anne, was in a Boutelle morning class the day before her baby was born, and returned ten days later, rarin' to go.

Grace Y., 78: This spunky lady hobbled in at age 71, using a cane, hardly able to walk. In a few months she discarded her cane. Within a year, the doctors agreed to do replacement surgery on one hip because of her fine overall condition. She recovered with remarkable speed. A year later they did similar surgery on her other hip. She continues her Boutelle natural-actions, and while on a trip at age 78 she wrote to me enthusiastically, "I'm walking all the beaches in Portugal without any trouble!"

CHECKLIST OF UNNATURAL "EXERCISES" AND ACTIVITIES

• *"Exercise" and calisthenics programs,* created basically for the *male* body, often force female muscles and joints UNnaturally and harmfully. Essentials such as correct body alignment are neglected, resulting in strained muscles, back troubles, other painful injuries, and potentially harmful body wear and tear.

• *Ballet, dance, and gymnastic movements* force muscles for extreme external responses. Included are UNnatural exertions such as body splits, balancing on tip-toe, extreme leaps and extensions, which demand more than the body is constructed to perform. Dancers and gymnasts are beset with bruising, sprains and strained muscles, torn ligaments, and other injuries from doing what does *not* come naturally. If you are not training for a professional dance career, *beware of such exertions.*

• *Using weights, dumbbells, slantboards, apparatus and gadgets* is

UNnatural and can be damaging. Using weights and push-pull and other equipment often causes muscle abnormalities, inciting more injuries. Artificial devices such as slantboards, teeter-totters and motorized apparatus are questionable at best. Boutelle natural-actions use no other equipment than your own body, according to my proved Mother-Nature-knew-what-she-was-doing thesis. It's UNnatural to isolate and force separate parts of the body, often causing painful problems such as "tennis elbow," strains and sprains.

• *Jogging, running, sports* require all-over, inside-out conditioning with natural-actions *before* exerting your body strenuously. All-over, inside-out neuromuscular fitness is a *must* for safe, beneficial sports activity, to help prevent sprains, strains, torn ligaments, broken bones, and excessive wear and tear that may bring on heart attacks and permanent injury. You will enjoy recreational sports most, and perform best, by conditioning your body every day with regular and special natural-actions (see Chapter XI).

RESHAPING YOUR LIFE STYLE FOR THE BETTER

Whatever your age, you will be reshaping your lifestyle, without strain, as you become consciously and fully fit rather than semi-fit or worse. You will raise your energy and endurance levels remarkably in everything you do, whether improving your sports skills or wielding a broom, playing paddle tennis or gardening—in short, in every move you make. Learning "daily living natural-actions" (Chapter X) will help you handle everyday tasks more easily and safely, all-important to help avoid injuries and improve your total well-being.

Basically, the Boutelle Method of Lifetime Fitness is a different, scientific, enjoyable natural-action therapy proved by over 10,000 women to be far more effective in providing immediate improvement and enduring fitness; it is so unique that it has been granted U.S. Patent No. 29,116 and trademark recognition. As a simple clue, try pronouncing the hard-sounding word, "EX-ER-CISE," as contrasted with the smooth-flowing word, "natural." Similarly, smooth-running, rhythmic Boutelle natural-actions contrast with the overstraining, uncoordinated manipulations of old-fashioned, boring "exercise" routines.

Furthermore, I have always been totally opposed to the dangerous but still prevalent concept that "It's not doing you any good unless it *hurts*." Realize that it's *how* you move that counts, not how fast or how hard you move. My firm rule is that if you ever feel the slightest pain or strain, tell yourself instantly, "Whoa, STOP, that's enough"—and rest before you go on, or try again tomorrow.

As you attain neuromuscular fitness, you will learn new, quicker, smoother response and movement patterns in everything you do— to replace old, awkward, weakening practices. You will feel better and brighter since your improved nerve and muscle systems are not separate entities but are connected to the mind, and affect how you feel mentally as well as physically.

HOW NATURAL-ACTIONS WORK BEST FOR WOMEN

From the start of my studies and development as a movement specialist, it became increasingly clear to me that exercise programs were designed by men for a *man's* body. Routines then, and still today, were planned primarily for male armed forces training and for "jocks" and musclebusters rather than for the average individual, and definitely *not* for women.

After her first class, a student told me, "Other women's classes I've attended are like taking setting-up exercises in the army." I determined to change all that, to make activity for women not only effective but fun.

In working out the Boutelle Method, I took into account the special and specific measurable physical distinctions between the sexes in body build, weight distribution, and other important factors. Although individuals vary, of course, *average* male and female bodies differ in the following ways:

• *Shoulders of males* are generally wider than those of females, while women are broader at the hips. Males on the whole are more muscular.

Albrecht Dürer: *Fall of Man*. THE METROPOLITAN MUSEUM OF ART, FLETCHER FUND, 1919.

• *Great contrast in pelvic formation:* A narrower, tighter pelvis helps males run faster. The female pelvis is broader, more flexible for specific functions such as giving birth; the female pelvis also is angled differently, causing the figure to jut out more at the rear.

• *Average female trunk* is longer than the male torso, compared with length of legs; it is also fleshier than the male's.

• *Rib structure* is generally shorter and more rounded in females, usually resulting in a comparatively narrower waist.

• *Women's arms*, on average, are shorter than men's in proportion to the trunk; women's elbows are higher due to a shorter humerus bone (between shoulder and elbow joints).

• *There are also many other all-important differences* in muscle, bone, and skull size, weight of the heart and other organs, as well as an obvious contrast in breasts.

BASIC BODY DIFFERENCES BETWEEN FEMALE AND MALE—THE FOUNDATION OF THE BOUTELLE METHOD

As you can see clearly in *"The Fall of Man,"* the art masterpiece by Dürer, there are many vital differences between male and female physical forms, a fact largely ignored by exercise, calisthenics, and fitness programs.

Diagrams on figure outlines invariably show men wider at top, narrower at hips—in almost reverse proportion to women. Nevertheless, fitness programs generally apply male-proportioned exercise to female bodies, UNnaturally, and often injuriously.

Here is just one of the dramatic structural differences between female and male bodies: Note greater width of pelvis bone and aperture in the average female as compared with the male. Obviously, a fitness program for women must be designed specifically for women, as is the Boutelle Method.

FEMALE PELVIS (FRONT)

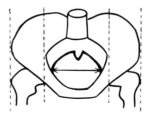

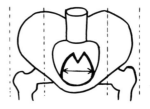

MALE PELVIS (FRONT)

Clearly, it doesn't make good sense or the most effective body conditioning to offer women fitness programs designed for male bodies. Therefore I eliminated straining, jerky, inappropriate and overly demanding, often harmful exertions (wrong for men, too). Step by step I created smooth, rhythmic, graceful natural-actions tailored for women—a crucial difference. For example, no push-ups, since women are not constructed with the big shoulder muscles to do customary male push-ups; instead you will do the Boutelle "Kitten Curl" (Chapter VII).

You are never asked to do anything awkwardly or abruptly, as I stress the necessity of all your movements' "running smooth." The joints in your body, as in any piece of machinery, must run smoothly in order to run well, to endure. You must not overload machinery—or your body. You condition your body *safely* as you learn *safety-flow transitions*, for example, moving you smoothly from one natural-action to another, an exclusive feature. You attain a more graceful feminine appearance and vitality, never a hard, muscled, overexercised look.

A PROGRAM BASED ON THOROUGH, VARIED EXPERIENCE

The Boutelle Method is the outgrowth of my years of study and teaching in the fields of movement eduction. This includes dance, body mechanics, and neuromuscular fitness. In my graduate work at Columbia, I produced a research paper on movement. Through the years I became an acknowledged *movement specialist* as I studied, tested, and created innovations that promote good health and well-being especially for the female body and psyche. For instance, I patterned some flowing movements on my dance experience, but eliminated potentially harmful ballet and gymnastic dance actions which involve UNnatural, excessive exertions.

The nucleus of the method was a class in "Movement Exploration" that I devised and taught women at Marymount College, Tarrytown, New York. This was so successful in developing immediate and lifetime fitness skills that I was asked to present a program for women of all ages at the White Plains, New York, YWCA. This one course has expanded in relatively few years to thousands of women annually in many classes in the area, spreading to many communities and to other parts of the country. The remarkable growth is due to one basic fact: Women, delighted with their own thrilling results, tell others who join and become boosters.

Thanks to *all-over* conditioning, many students have reported that they have survived skiing and other accidents without serious injury because of their improvement in neuromuscular fitness, grace, and body control. Peggy T. said, a month after she joined my program, "I used to be an awkward clown. I was always tripping over things and bruising myself, bumping into people. But I don't do that any more. As you taught, my body is now properly aligned. I feel well balanced, even graceful now, and I love it."

So will you love your realigned appearance and performance.

ACTIVATING YOUR 632 MUSCLES

It is vital for you to understand a little about muscular function in relation to your best total functioning. There are about 632 muscles in your body (anatomists' numbers vary slightly)—in fact, we are all nearly two-thirds muscles; many we never use due to inactivity. *The body demands activity.* Muscles must be used, or they deteriorate, negatively affecting how you look, feel, and function. Just flexing your muscles, as in usual exercise programs, is not enough.

Actually the average person, unfit from my viewpoint, uses fewer than half her muscles to any significant extent daily. The hundreds of muscles that aren't used turn into flab and don't lend support to your body. No wonder you hear people complain frequently, "I'm so-o-o tired. . . ." But when you say you are tired, where is the tiredness? It's *neuromuscular*, in your nerves and muscles primarily. When your muscles are improved to move and function smoothly and easily all day long, you are counteracting tension and tiredness, and acting to relieve and overcome those debilitating conditions.

Improper but common *shallow breathing* also tends to make you feel tired. You will appreciate the energizing difference after your first easygoing Boutelle session as *you learn how to breathe properly*, at rest and while moving. You will feel repeated uplift quickly because your circulatory and respiratory systems will have been stimulated correctly, thoroughly.

You'll say that "it's so good to move" as the new neuromuscular release exhilarates you mentally and physically. In effect you will also be putting energy in the bank. You will wake up from sleep with a vital feeling of *stored energy*, not exhaustion.

You'll realize as soon as you begin natural-actions that you benefit from many desirable advances. You don't use any equipment—no dumbbells, no gadgets, no weights to lift. *Your own body is all the equipment you need.* Weight-lifting, for example, tends to build abnormalities into muscles, and in turn invites more injury.

In contrast, natural-actions are fluid motions that train your body to stretch and flow in one long, continuous, seamless line as you move, walk, bend, work, engage in sports, whatever you do. They help you develop what I call *rhythmic pacing*. Nervous and physical strain and stress ease off. Tight muscles relax. Tension is relieved.

Running smoothly, you will experience and enjoy invigorating neuromuscular flow from now on as your body is awakened and used fully and all over—in your daily session and throughout your waking hours.

THE FOUR BOUTELLE STEPS TO LIFETIME FITNESS

Conditioning your body beautifully results not from reading about it but from *doing*, of course. However, I believe it will be helpful to you, as it is to the individuals in my classes, to take a few minutes to understand exactly what the Boutelle Method is designed to do for you, step by step, and what it will accomplish with your full cooperation. Please note each element in detail. The Boutelle Method—

1. *realigns your body for smoothest functioning.* This is vital because no matter how well various parts of your body are working separately, your entire body must be realigned properly for best all-

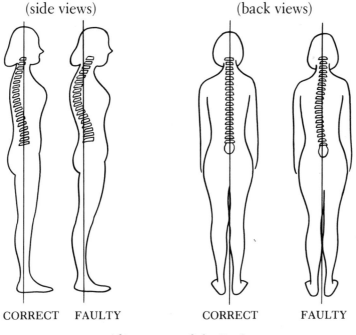

(side views)		(back views)	
CORRECT	FAULTY	CORRECT	FAULTY

Alignment of the Body
(drawings based on actual photographs)

over performance. Think of this as similar to having the motor, wheels, and all parts of your car realigned in an all-over checkup. This should be done at least annually for most automobiles, but the great majority of individuals go on creaking more, year after year, without getting needed body realignment. Note in the simplified diagram illustrations how badly the entire body can be thrown off proper balance by faulty alignment. Your daily program acts to align your body correctly for most attractive posture, ease of movement, and your improved total functioning and health.

2. *improves your muscle tone (elasticity or tonus)*. Boutelle natural-action conditioning firms your all-over muscular structure to support your bones, joints, and entire torso for your most efficient, easy, tension-free movement in all situations. This can be compared to tightening all the screws, nuts and bolts in realigning a car for smooth, balanced and friction-free operation.

3. *develops and improves neuromuscular coordination*. As your body alignment is correctly adjusted, you will be substituting new muscle and nerve responses for old, debilitating habits. With nerves and muscles coordinating well instead of raggedly, the rapid improvement in your functioning will surprise and delight you. It's as though a car which is subject to misfiring, slowing up, and other recurrent problems is given a fine major tune-up that balances all systems and functions so that it hums along perfectly.

4. *builds vitality and endurance*. Your use of Boutelle natural-actions in your daily living will increase your vigor and stamina to the best it can be for your chronological and physiological age. That is the very desirable, realistic goal of your conditioning program: to raise you to your highest personal neuromuscular attainment and keep you there from now on, no matter at what age you begin.

WHY NEUROMUSCULAR FITNESS IS A MUST FOR ALL

I must insert a personal note to explain my almost fanatical emphasis on neuromuscular lifetime fitness for you, for everyone. My husband, a high-powered executive, a "weekend athlete," kept promising me that he would join my conditioning program "someday, when I can find the time." About to assume a top position in a big business, under tremendous pressure and tension, he died shockingly one night of a sudden heart attack, at a relatively early age.

When I adjusted after a period of time, I determined to make it my lifework to urge and help every woman and man to attain top neuromuscular fitness to help prevent such tragedies, as well as to get the most out of living. I developed the simple, easy, do-it-yourself program in this book so that nobody would have an excuse to be unfit since a session that moves all 632 muscles takes only a few minutes a day. If you cannot afford to give that much time to improving your health, then you are saying that you cannot afford to live to your full capacity and potential . . . and your full years.

I implore you to ponder three words that stab deep into me when I see friends who are not as fit and healthy as they can be because they don't care: "What a waste!" What a waste when unfit individuals are stricken and die before their time due to coronary and other often preventable disorders. What a waste if you let yourself be dragged down day after day by flab and sluggishness . . . and permit yourself to look, feel, and function below your top attainable capacity. *What a waste!* Please join me in changing all that for you and yours. The nicest thing you can do for yourself and the people who love you is to take care of you.

Although the Boutelle Method is designed for the female body specifically, you will see in a later section (Chapter XIII) that some of the natural-actions have been altered and varied for men, to conform to their basic structural differences. I developed these natural-actions for "His and Her Classes," which had been requested urgently by wives who were worried about their husbands' being unfit, flabby, risking heart attacks and other health dangers. Physicians, executives, and others who have taken these classes for several years at this writing endorse the effectiveness of the *male* Boutelle program in boosting their fitness, energy, and total well-being.

Special Reminder: Since you don't need any special equipment (no weights, no apparatus), you can enjoy your daily fitness session wherever you go—in hotel rooms, visiting a friend's home. You "carry" Lifetime Fitness with you wherever you are, anywhere in the world.

II

Start with These Basic Boutelle Natural-Actions

I was waiting in my car for the red light to change one day when an auto pulled up alongside me. The driver, one of my students, called out, "Think IN, Jane! Think UP, Jane!" She laughed and drove away as the light changed to green.

Those words have become amusing catchphrases for the people in my classes, and they will for you too. I want you to say them aloud and keep them in mind so that the actions become a natural part of your more attractive bearing in everything you do: "Think IN . . . Think UP." Sitting, standing, lying down, those four little words coupled with their actions will keep you looking, feeling, and functioning better—*no question about it*. If, instead, you slump while sitting, standing, or walking, your shape goes out of shape, and sags and bulges appear—which disappear when you think IN, think UP.

Please try this right now before you read further:

Think IN means to pull your abdomen IN as far as you can toward your spine and lower back. As you sit, *think IN:* pull in your middle, not jerkily or forcefully, but slowly and comfortably so that you can keep sitting that way without excessive effort. Direct your abdomen to *flow* back toward your spine . . .

Think IN

Think UP

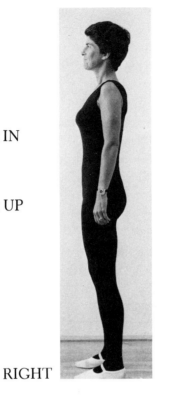

RIGHT

WRONG!

Sitting—RIGHT

Sitting—WRONG

Now, at the same time, *think UP:* Slowly, naturally, stretch your body up from your pelvis as you take a deep breath and stretch up from your seat right through the top of your head—as though a string attached to your head is pulling you up.

Do you feel and see distinct improvement in your figure at once as you combine thinking IN with thinking UP? Using the tape measure will prove to you that you can actually take inches off your middle at once when you think IN, think UP, and develop the habit. Thinking IN flattens your abdomen, while thinking UP lifts your chest, straightens your back and neck, and adds new grace and beauty to your posture, including a lovelier lifted bosom contour. I have seen this remarkable figure correction thousands of times with my students.

When you think IN and think UP, you are thinking *fitness* and suiting your actions to the thought. A vital part of Boutelle Method effectiveness for you depends on your thinking "fitness" every wak-

WRONG: *Most women push a shopping cart slumped over, bringing on fatigue and back muscle pains, and lasting troubles.*

RIGHT: *Standing in straight Boutelle alignment, elbows in, your body is comfortable and moves smoothly and easily—and looks more attractive.*

ing hour until it soon becomes an unconscious part of you wherever you are, whatever you are doing.

When you are standing in a supermarket checkout line . . . walking and perhaps pushing a carriage or carrying a package . . . sitting in a bus, train, plane, or car . . . working at a desk or eating, chatting, reading, or watching TV . . .standing at the kitchen sink, or almost anywhere—think IN and think UP, and you will be promoting your fitness now and for your lifetime.

IMMEDIATE IMPROVEMENT

As you think IN and think UP in everything you do, and enjoy your ten-minute natural-actions session daily, your mirror and your friends will tell you that you *look better* as you develop and maintain the graceful movements and sure, zestful step of the wide-awake body . . .

You will *feel better* because you are building strong abdominal muscles that will support your more erect, aligned spine. With this proper neuromuscular support, chronic aches and pains tend to disappear. You will sleep better, awake refreshed, deal better with the stresses of everyday living . . .

You will *function better* as you develop stronger heart muscles, lungs that perform at full capacity, and improved circulatory, respiratory, and digestive systems that work more smoothly, easily, and efficiently . . .

You will *perform better* as your muscles and nerves combine to produce smoother, speedier, better coordinated neuromuscular responses to daily demands. You will gain relief from tension, and you will find that you can work and play harder and longer without getting exhausted. You will bounce back more quickly after illness and setbacks. The improvement in your basic, all-over neuromuscular condition *can make the difference between life or death* after a destructive incident or accident.

One student told me, "Jane, I even *smile* easier and brighter because I feel so good!" Dr. Michael DeBakey, noted specialist, stated that with moderate activity, " . . . circulation is kept going in a better way, the heart responds better; you think better because there is more oxygen to the brain."

CONDITIONS YOU INSIDE-OUT

Natural-actions move *inside-out*, from deep in your respiratory and circulatory systems, helping to reduce and control high blood pressure, and build resistance against heart attacks and many other common problems. Your body needs these deep inside-out *natural*, not forced, movements to repair and build up nerves and muscles therapeutically. Furthermore, massage, vibrating machines, and other methods applied from the outside to the passive body don't even begin to provide the deep, lasting benefits needed.

In each ten-minute daily session, you will activate all 632 muscles and every joint, to help build and keep your muscular structure smooth and firm, not overdeveloped. The resulting firm conditioning gives the best possible support for the entire skeletal structure to help prevent mishaps, neck, shoulder, and lower back pains, and other common afflictions. By firming flabby, fatty muscles all over, and improving your posture greatly, *you firm inches away quickly*. The inside-out method improves your internal systems deeply.

It's a shocking fact that about 60 percent of women have *circulatory* problems, indicated often by cold hands and feet. Natural-actions not only improve circulation but also work deep into the digestive tract. Digestion is a muscular process, and individuals frequently develop problems because they lack muscle tone in the digestive tract. My program builds up the muscle response you need all over.

CONDITIONING A MUST FOR SPORTS, "FUN ACTIVITIES"

I endorse and encourage your participation in sports and recreational activities, but must warn that your body should be conditioned properly all over *beforehand*, and that sports alone don't condition the body fully. Without essential all-over, inside-out muscular support, you cannot function most safely and at your potential best in fun activities such as tennis, golf, bowling, and swimming—as well as in daily living. An area golf champion, Harriet B., told me, "Your program helped cut strokes from my score by conditioning me all over and improving my fitness and coordination—I ought to give you my trophies!"

Please understand this clearly: There is no way you can change your skeletal frame from short to tall, or lengthen or shorten your bones (short of surgery). But you can firm and improve your body's appearance and functioning for sports and better living, simply by following my instructions. Isn't it worth a daily ten-minute session, and a lifetime of thinking fitness, to be healthier and more alive from now on, with increasing benefits week after week?

Developing this everyday pattern of neuromuscular uplift helps remarkably to retard the physical and neurological effects of aging. You will even walk better, as I teach you through "analytical walking" (Chapter X) to replace the usual faulty knee-pushing movement with a graceful, springy stride from the hip. You will walk through life with far more energy and joy. A student in her forties said, "My husband told me yesterday that I now walk like a lively eighteen-year-old."

NOT FLABBY, NOT IRON-MUSCLED

"Sponge-cake firmness": My students have been amused by this phrase and delighted when they become "sponge-cake firm"—as they develop a springy musculature rather than a mushy-soft or hardened one. You know what that means if you have ever baked or touched a perfect sponge cake, and how desirable that springiness is in order to have the most beautiful body and bearing that you personally can develop. Your body will not be flabby any longer, not iron-muscled, but sponge-cake firm, your flesh gently resistant to the touch.

No more "layer-cake back" or "marshmallow territory": Both of these undesirable conditions are due to flab, and are familiar to every woman as a potential threat if not an actuality, no matter how thin she may be. "Layer-cake back" refers to those rounded rolls of flesh, like cake layers, that tend to appear, especially in the female figure, at the lower back above the buttocks.

"Marshmallow territory" describes the mushy swells in certain areas which afflict even a slim woman if she is flabby rather than firm. For example, touch your flesh just in front of the armpit at your upper chest; is it sponge-cake firm—or marshmallow soft?

Build your own "muscle girdle": Unattractive layer-cake back and all your areas of marshmallow territory will tighten up, smooth out and disappear as your body is re-aligned and you stand erect, supported by your new firming girdle—your *muscle girdle*. Alice R. had a typical bulging tummy when she joined my classes. I pointed to her stomach and said, "We'll soon get rid of that soft marshmallow territory."

She sighed, "But I can't keep my stomach in."

"You will—when you build your own muscle girdle."

Some time later, she told me happily, "Look, that stomach bulge is gone. My dress fit so smoothly today that I gave the credit to my panty girdle—until I realized that I wasn't wearing any. My new 'muscle girdle' was doing the job."

No matter how flabby you may be right now, you can usually build your own firm girdle of muscles—and throw away your panty girdles. Muscles are not like elastic bands that lose shape permanently when stretched too much. *Your muscles can always come back with natural-action conditioning.* How soon depends on your personal condition now, and on how faithfully you follow the Boutelle Method.

You must maintain that springy sponge-cake firmness by adhering to the program, because *muscles demand movement* to stay toned in top condition. You cannot store fitness; you must move your muscles regularly and properly to maintain your beautifully firmed figure.

IMPORTANT GUIDELINES AND TIPS

• *Use your tape measure rather than the scale* to check the trimming and slimming of your figure through the Boutelle Method. Natural-actions firm and tighten your muscular structure, and thus trim off flab so that you can *take inches off,* measured by the tape. And you can *drop a full dress size or more* without losing much in pounds on the scale. With inches firmed off, you can see as well as feel the wonderful difference, whether you are basically thin or overweight. However, to drop many pounds of fat, go on an effective reducing diet; you can't count on body conditioning alone.

• *Don't overexert—if it hurts, STOP at once!* That's a primary, in-flexible rule of the Boutelle Method. I condemn physical training instructors who urge people to force and strain beyond their capacities at any time. That's not only wrong, it's dangerous and can be injurious. Please note this carefully and never forget it: Pain, weakness, and quivering muscles are signals that tell you to halt *immediately.*

With Boutelle conditioning you cannot overexert unless you are not following directions and are moving your body incorrectly, abruptly, or jerkily. My natural-actions must *flow* rhythmically, smoothly, comfortably. Keep in mind as you move through your daily sessions, and in all actions, my two-word guideline: *Run smooth.*

This safety factor is part of one of my proudest achievements—having a number of pregnant women in my classes (continuing with their doctors' permission always, of course). Many enjoy my pelvic tilt and other natural-actions right up to a day or two before giving birth. Then they come back to class soon after, radiant about how well their bodies functioned while pregnant, during birth, and afterward. They report compliments from their physicians on their superb physical conditioning.

I'm against forcing repeated exertions, rigidly instructed by others, doing "so many this" and "so many that" regardless of how you feel. Part of neuromuscular fitness is knowing yourself, understanding your personal capacities and limitations. In my classes, some women stop and rest in position when they feel they have reached their limits, while others continue their natural-actions. Then, after a pause, those who have stopped may pick up again and go on. The Boutelle credo for you is "to make me a better me," not a superstar, which you cannot be if it isn't in you.

I tell you repeatedly, as I tell my classes: *Don't overdo—you are not competing with anyone.* A competitive spirit just adds undesirable tension and stress, which Boutelle conditioning is designed to eliminate. Your only concern, like mine, is your *personal* top conditioning. The only prize you are trying for is to gain your maximum vitality, vigor and endurance today, and lifetime fitness from now on. That makes you a winner.

• *Follow instructions exactly.* Using the Boutelle Method must always keep you calm, at ease. You avoid certain common "calisthenics" errors that are not only undesirable but dangerous. Going through the rhythmic natural-actions when standing, for instance, your feet must never be tight together as some others instruct incorrectly. Instead, your feet are a few inches apart—wherever they are most supportive naturally, and thoroughly comfortable for *you.* No jerky actions ever. No excessive speed-up . . . *slow movements build endurance.* No exaggerated, straining, *extra-deep* knee bends; you will learn smooth, *modified* knee actions. No overexerting forward bends, such as touching your toes with knees stiff, which may cause severe back trouble. No improper stiff-kneed leg raises, which may pull the spine badly out of alignment.

• *Forget about "isotonic" and "isometric" labels* in performing natural-actions. Mostly you will be doing a combination of isotonic and isometric movements, but there is so much confusion about the terms that they should not concern you. Just do all the actions in proper alignment . . . think IN and think UP . . . follow directions carefully . . . and you will be moving and using muscles properly for effective isotonic/isometric conditioning—no limp, unproductive motions.

• *Never ignore personal neuromuscular problems, or any disorders or illnesses.* Without fail, before beginning this or any other activity program, get an overall checkup and full approval from your doctor, along with regular medical checkups for the rest of your life. I am proud of the fact that my classes include female and male physicians, their husbands and wives, and many individuals referred to me specifically by their doctors.

PROGRAMS TO FIT YOU PERSONALLY

Nobody is permitted to start out like a house afire in the Boutelle Method. You attune your ten-minute daily session to your personal neuromuscular condition when you begin. Then you advance at your own pace to more demanding natural-actions as your capacities expand. You gradually increase the speed and number of repetitions of a particular natural-action as you improve your muscle tone and coordination.

First, you test your neuromuscular fitness by checking yourself with the three Self-Tests in Chapter VI. You get a feeling of what your condition is at the start, and at what pace you should proceed. You apply these same tests two weeks later, and you will discover how wonderfully you have advanced in improving your alignment, coordination, and endurance.

Second, you begin with the "A" Alpha Program, just as alpha begins the alphabet. You start here, no matter how athletic or fit you think you may be. You must begin gradually. Even though you may think that they are not demanding enough for you, you will enjoy the easygoing "A" natural-actions. Remember, they are moving and using all 632 muscles in your body (many of which you may not have used for a long time), and conditioning you properly all over, inside-out—aligning and firming your body, building vigor and endurance.

Third, you advance to the "B" Best Program as your fitness improves steadily and inevitably. "B" is for the best you can be. There is no need or benefit for anyone to go beyond that. (Of course, if you are a specialized professional athlete, you will be getting specific extra training elsewhere.) The "B" program will promote and maintain your personal top neuromuscular fitness for the rest of your better life—that's "lifetime fitness."

Fourth, if you have any illness, disorder, disability, you belong in my "M" Medical Referral Program. In your medical checkup, your physician will inform you of your limitations (please show him or her this book). We provide instructions for individuals with back troubles or arthritis, those who have had a mastectomy, and others. These are specially created additions and modifications of Boutelle basic natural-actions.

Many "M" students eventually are able to go on to the "A" and "B" programs. Some who have come to my classes with canes have been able to throw them away after a while. Helen G., in her fifties, was afflicted with a congenital hip disorder that inhibited bending; after a month of natural-actions, she said, "Jane, do you know how marvelous it feels to be able to bend enough to cut your own toenails again?"

A gallant woman of 38, Mary W., was referred to my classes by her doctor after her mastectomy. She came in listless and defeated, feeling crippled. She told me, "Your program picked me up in a way that I couldn't believe was possible. You brought me along slowly and steadily, so I stopped feeling like a misfit. Now that I've advanced to the 'B' program, I can do everything the others do—in my daily living too. It sounds impossible, but I've never before had this exhilarating sense of wide-awake fitness, even before my surgery." (I feel honored that special-care organizations as well as physicians have referred patients for rehabilitation through the Boutelle Method.)

In later sections, you will also find natural-actions to firm and smooth *problem spots*—shoulders, arms, midsection, hips, buttocks, thighs—effective only after you have developed basic neuromuscular fitness.

To increase your sports proficiency and enjoyment, you will find specific natural-actions to help improve your scores and your fun in tennis, golf, bowling, and other recreational activities. And you will like looking better as your figure firms and you move more smoothly and gracefully, thanks to your better alignment and coordination.

For men only, modifications and special basic natural-actions are provided for the male body, created to build deep, inside-out lifetime fitness and to help him prevent heart attacks and other disorders.

YOUR PART OF THE BARGAIN

Please promise yourself and us that you will follow through faithfully for at least one week of the Boutelle Method—day by day, not skipping a day's session. Indisputable health statistics affirm that most people—probably you, too—are operating at far below their physical potential. We're not going to throw a lot of terrifying facts at you. Instead we prefer to accentuate the positive, to prove to you how much better you can look and feel and function from now on, fully awakened and alive with new energy, endurance, grace. You will prove it best for yourself within one short week of your program.

This will be a *lifetime* book for you, as useful to you in ten and more years as right now. Our mutual goal is *mens sana in corpore sano*—what I call in effect "neuromuscular lifetime fitness." It is, as Homer called it, "the greatest blessing for man" (and woman!). The essayist Locke summed it up: "A sound mind in a sound body is a short but full description of a happy state in this world."

III
Three Goals for Improving Your Figure and Fitness

GOAL ONE: CORRECT BODY ALIGNMENT

Realignment of your body will be the foundation of your looking, moving, and functioning better. Before you start your daily program, it will help you to understand a little more about your anatomy—exactly what happens and why when you move your body with Boutelle natural-actions. A lot of your past misconceptions about "exercise," as dictated by others, will be destroyed for all time—and a good thing, too.

For example, when you were a child you were probably told by gym teachers and other well-meaning adults, "Pull your shoulders back." That's a Victorian expression we'd like to have abolished forever. What happens when you throw your shoulders back forcefully? It puts stress on weak pelvic muscles (at base of spine) . . . the lumbar spine arches (at back and sides between lowest ribs and pelvis) . . . and the abdominal (belly) muscles bounce out desirably.

Instead of pulling your shoulders back forcibly, think IN, think UP—this time *standing* (see Chapter II). Pull IN your abdominal muscles toward your lower back . . . as you stretch UPward from your pelvis while taking a deep breath . . . standing with feet a few inches apart naturally, hands comfortably at your sides, palms facing body. Hold this posture as you exhale, blowing air out forcibly through your mouth—all the while thinking IN, thinking UP.

When you perform this natural-action correctly, your shoulders will be back automatically, aligned correctly over you hip sockets. Try it again now, preferably while looking in a full-length mirror. See how beautifully your shoulders and upper body are aligned?

Harness Your Shoulders

I compare the grouping of shoulder muscles to the straps of a harness in that they are intended to keep the shoulders under firm control. Lamentably, most people have let their bodies deteriorate into a very loose harness which causes the shoulders to roll forward in an unattractive, weakening slouch or slump. You must and can correct this condition of rounded shoulders by doing this:

You will have the correct body alignment that Jane Boutelle teaches in her classes. Here, shoulder and hip sockets are in alignment, supporting the upper body most attractively and comfortably.

Back view: Shoulder sockets in alignment horizontally; shoulder and hip sockets in alignment vertically; the result is beautiful, healthful posture.

First, feel your "pectoralis (chest) strap" by placing fingers of your right hand just in front of your left armpit on your chest; usually instead of a firm muscle strap you will feel soft, flabby "marshmallow territory," as noted earlier.

This condition bothers many women because a roll of flesh hangs out when they wear bathing suits or sleeveless dresses. This defect, along with rounded shoulders, can be corrected by tightening the lower strap of the "pectoralis major," the large fan-shaped muscle located in the front (anterior) chest wall. (Yor don't have to know anatomy, since you can count on your Boutelle program to condition you properly and correct those defects.) I call the flabby area at the armpits the "pectoral pin points," and I urge you, as I have told my classes for years: *"Push IN Your Pectoral Pins!"*

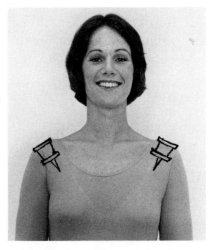

"PUSHPINS"

Basic Shoulder Natural-Actions

To do this natural-action right now, imagine that you have a large pushpin located just in front of each armpit (see photo). As you inhale deeply through your nose, *push in on your pins* (keep arms at sides, not touching your shoulders). Exhale slowly through your mouth, blowing out, but keep the pins in place. Do that simple natural-action many times a day, whenever you think of it.

You will relieve shoulder ache instantly with a few repetitions of this action. Soon your muscle straps will become supportive, since your shoulders will be firmly harnessed. The unsightly rolls of flesh will disappear. Your posture will be more attractive since your shoulders are back naturally as you keep pushing your pectoral pins IN— soon you won't even be aware that you are doing it as it becomes your good habit. If your shoulders ever start to slump forward, remind yourself with the code word: *"Pushpins!"*

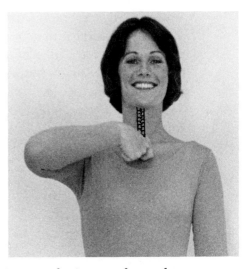

Basic Neck Natural-Action:
1. Zip Up Your Neck. 2. Smile

This simple little one-two natural-action taught in my classes has straightened necks properly, brought heads into correct alignment, eliminated the ungainly, unhealthy "looking-down syndrome," and helped relieve headaches for many. The looking-down syndrome puts undue stress on neck muscles. In turn, this causes many common headaches which are neuromuscular in origin.

Check yourself now in the mirror, holding your head as you usually do: Aren't you afflicted by the looking-down syndrome? Most activities we perform regularly cause us to look down. Mothers spend years looking down at little people, leaning over cribs and playpens, watching crawlers and toddlers. In doing household chores, you look down at sinks, and while preparing meals, dusting tables. Office workers look down as they work at desks. Students look down while reading and writing. Surgeons look down when they operate; dentists look "down in the mouth" all day long. Most drivers slouch over the steering wheel and look down at the road ahead.

To counteract the damage and destruction from so much necessary looking down, do this many times a day: *Zip up your neck . . . then smile.* The one-two natural-action is this easy and pleasant:

1. *Inhale* as you place your hand at the base of your neck at your throat, and as though you are pulling up a zipper, zip up your neck

so that your neck straightens and your chin comes up comfortably (see photo).

2. *Exhale* and smile—and tension and rigidity disappear as your smile relaxes your muscles in that area.

Repeat several times. You will find that with this quick one-two routine, your ears are placed naturally right over the shoulder muscle girdle instead of pushed forward, thus relieving and reducing neck tension. An extra reward from your improved posture comes when friends say, "You look wonderful—what have you been doing for yourself?" Besides, with all that practice, you will smile more easily, and that alone will make you (and others) feel better. Remember—(1) zip up your neck, (2) then smile—often every day, everywhere.

Standing in Correct Alignment

Together let us analyze your standing alignment from the front view, focusing on your whole body. Like most women when they come to the first class, you probably don't know how to stand for correct, supportive body alignment. For one thing, women have commonly been taught from childhood to stand with feet together to look "feminine and proper." This prevents correct alignment.

Think about it—babies *naturally* sit, crawl, and walk with legs a few inches apart, not tight together, for best support. If we were to draw a *straight line* (see photo) from the top of your leg over the center of the upper thigh, continuing the straight line over the center of the kneecap, *the legs would have to be apart*. How far apart is dictated by your own skeletal frame. I tell my classes, and now you, to stand and *place your heels directly under your hip sockets*.

Try it, preferably facing a full-length mirror. Your feet must be a few inches apart naturally (not a wide straddle), feet pointing straight ahead. Notice how you gain good *balance*, improved posture, and better body equilibrium as your weight is evenly distributed on your feet. You also get improved arch support, and quicker "reaction time" as you move your body from this solid stance.

Remember to stand this natural way always, feet comfortably and gracefully apart, in everything you do, as you think IN, think UP.

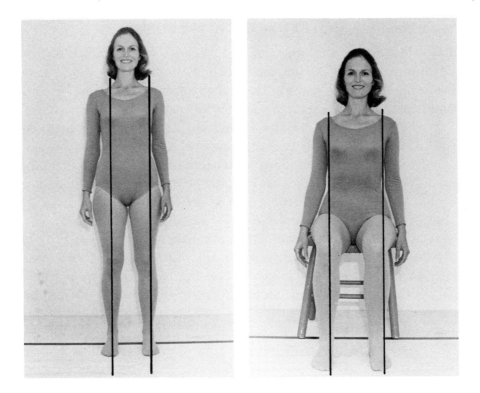

Sitting in Correct Alignment

Here's a sitting lesson from a frontal view: Sit on a hard chair or stool, feet set against the floor a few inches apart naturally, pointing straight forward. Again, think IN, pulling your abdominal muscles against the lower back; think UP from the pelvis. Now your ears are directly over your shoulders, and your shoulders are in a straight line over your hip sockets—naturally.

If, instead, you slouch in an easy chair as most people do, your lower (sacral and lumbar) spine is arched in a straining, stressful, unnatural curve. Over a period of time, this can and often does create extreme pain in the lower back, the too-well-known and long-suffered "lower back syndrome" (does it hurt even to hear the phrase?).

To help prevent and counteract *lower back pain*, realize that the pelvic girdle consists of a single bone, the *os innomatum* or "nameless" bone. The bottom surface of this bone contains two big bulges which you can feel when you sit in alignment. As you sit now, reach down, lean forward a little, and feel those hard bony bulges underneath, one with each hand, right at the bottom of your seat. I have taken the liberty of naming these the "sitting bones," and I constantly exhort my classes and you: *"Sit up on your sitting bones!"*

When you think IN, think UP, and sit on your sitting bones, you activate the building block of the spine, the *erector spinae* muscle, along with a complex series of muscles that support the spinal column. That is why you must always observe the simple natural-action of perching up on your sitting bones—when sitting in any type of chair, on a bench, or ledge, in a car, everywhere, every day.

That correct sitting alignment alone can work wonders to help prevent and relieve a tired back. Sitting otherwise can throw your back and body out of alignment—and that can spell *serious trouble.*When you notice your improved physical condition, you will be grateful for the rest of your life that you have learned to "sit up on your sitting bones."

From Sitting to Standing

When you go from sitting to standing, do it the correct, safe Boutelle way. Read the directions carefully, and adhere to them always. Don't slump or lurch forward to get up, risking back injury and looking awkward. Instead, do this: Keep your correct sitting alignment with feet a few inches apart and pointing straight forward . . . back erect . . . and *push your heels against the floor as you lift* . . . first lifting your sitting bones . . . then lifting your pelvis . . . keeping your shoulders relaxed, pectoral pins in, no slouching.

Going from sitting to standing this correct, easy way, your leg muscles will lift you upward smoothly, safely, gracefully. You will be standing well supported, your body in proper alignment to move into action. Practice this sitting-to-standing natural-action a few times now—and from now on.

Important Driving Lesson

Here's a valuable, essential tip when driving your car: When you seat yourself behind the wheel—sitting up on your sitting bones, pushpins in, neck zipped up—adjust your rear view mirror for a perfect, centered view of the scene behind you.

As you drive a while, look into the rear view mirror periodically. If you find that you are reaching to readjust the mirror for a perfect view, that's your reminder signal that you have slumped back on your spine and are probably slouching at the wheel. Readjust your *sitting posture* correctly, rather than your mirror: up on your sitting bones . . . pushpins in . . . neck zipped up —and *smile*.

GOAL TWO: NEUROMUSCULAR TONING AND COORDINATION

We're sure it will help you as a thinking person to adhere to the program faithfully if you understand a few of the basics about *how muscles and nerves operate*, for we want you to realize fully your need for *neuromuscular* fitness. Muscles may be likened to screws that hold our bones together. Each muscle performs a highly specialized task. Your muscles are made of fibers, each governed by its own nerve ending. Obviously your muscles could not operate without your central nervous system. When you improve your musculature, your nervous system benefits too.

Each muscle has its own fuel supply—arteries and veins carry blood through its fibers, which in turn act like pumps to keep your blood flow running smoothly. If your muscle fibers lack the strength to pump your blood supply effectively, your circulatory system runs inefficiently and may even break down. *This forces your main pump, the heart muscle, to work overtime, often with destructive results.*

I cannot emphasize enough that muscles are made to move, must move to maintain the proper amount of tonus, the elastic quality found in healthy muscles. When they are kept neuromuscularly well-toned, muscles perform more efficiently and effectively as they contract and extend. The individual who lacks muscle tone is more likely to be "uptight," as she is forced to "run on nervous energy" to meet many of life's daily demands—and she tends to burn out quickly.

Your brief anatomy lesson is almost finished: Realize that most muscles work in *pairs*, one pulling against the other and dividing the work load. In the well-coordinated person, the muscle pairs operate smoothly, one with the other, in performing a given assignment with muscular agility and smooth skeletal movement. For top coordination, it is absolutely necessary to maintain muscle tone through purposeful natural-actions.

When your daily chores and activities do not provide sufficient contraction and expansion of muscle pairs, they lose elasticity, become flabby, and you tire easily. Flabby, weak muscles upset the nervous system, often causing people to nag, to become listless and depressed, to complain about "nerves"—all likely evidences of neuromuscular debilitation. Keep clearly in mind, that *flab* is due to underusing muscles, while *fat* occurs from overfeeding the body, including muscles. Boutelle neuromuscular conditioning counteracts flab and firms the body.

GOAL THREE: NEUROMUSCULAR ENDURANCE

Endurance is "lasting quality"—the power to withstand hardship and stress. It's a quality we all want and need for two primary reasons: (1) to have the stamina to function well daily and (2) to live as long as possible, healthfully and vigorously.

The general signs are promising since in the past century life expectancy for women has nearly doubled to beyond age 75 instead of death at a little more than 40. But you cannot expect to increase your personal life span if you choose to live in a state of below-par health and well-being by not activating your body machine sufficiently and properly.

You realize now that you cannot neglect your musculature and still justifiably complain of weariness after moderate physical exertion. You know that tiredness is *lack of neuromuscular energy*, which you will remedy. You have been informed that you cannot misuse your body all week and yet expect it to perform well and respond with strength and stamina in weekend sports or other demanding exertions. Working daily with natural-actions, you will build and maintain the foundation for improved and sustained performance.

HOW LONG WILL IT TAKE?

The question that I am often asked by beginning students may be in your mind now: "How long will it take me to attain my top neuro-muscular fitness?" I usually ask quietly in turn, "How long have you been insufficiently active and allowed your body to deteriorate to less that what it can and should be?"

In fact, you will start to feel improvement *from the first day* you begin this program. Your neuromuscular fitness will increase week by week as you go on, never pressing or overexerting but following directions correctly. It will be easy for you, as with thousands of my students, to perform your daily natural-actions year after year be-cause you will look, feel, and function so much better than before. That is your proved motivation, your built-in will power.

In summary, your Boutelle program, followed faithfully, will bring you all these life-saving, life-improving benefits:
1. Correct alignment, improve muscle tone, give you built-in endurance.
2. Help keep your nervous system in balance, under control.
3. Promote essential neuromuscular coordination.
4. Strengthen the heart muscle.
5. Help your circulatory, respiratory, and digestive systems to function effectively.
6. Help control weight and dimensions when teamed with proper eating habits.

The beginning of your more energetic, more rewarding life is now . . . and from now on . . .

IV

Learning Rhythmic-Flow Breathing for Lifetime Fitness

You probably don't know how to breathe right. Does that blunt challenge shock you? It should, because respiration—the seemingly simple process of breathing in and breathing out—is fundamental to your lifetime fitness. You are losing out every day if you don't breathe correctly, deeply, fully. Yet I have found with people of all ages joining my classes that *up to 90 percent don't know how to breathe properly at the start.* When they learn quickly, as you will, they gain new exhilaration and energy from every breath.

To understand the importance of correct breathing, realize that the human body has a marvelous combustion system which may be compared in a general way with the combustion mechanism in your car. The human system needs over 12,000 quarts of oxygen from the air per day (plus food) to produce power, and it expends carbon dioxide and water. A car's combustion system combines gasoline with oxygen from the air in proper ratio to produce power, and it expends carbon monoxide and water. You had better take as good care of your personal combustion system as that of your car.

You inhale air through your nose. The air is warmed and moistened in your body on its trip to your lungs. The lung linings store oxygen safely, keeping it moist and protected from damage and invasion by disease-producing organisms. Also, the linings transfer oxygen to the bloodstream, and then permit carbon dioxide to be blown out from the lungs with your next breath. In short, you *inhale* and breathe in oxygen, you *exhale* and breathe out carbon dioxide.

Right now you can and should improve your body's basically superb two-stroke in-out natural action as you breathe in through your nose and breathe out through your mouth. With correct, *deep*, *full breathing*, which will become your personal more efficient natural-action, you may as much as double your *vital lung capacity*, depending on your present condition. Boosting your supply of oxygen helps your system burn up food and calories more effectively (an aid in reducing overweight), acts to cut down risks from heart attack, and aids in improving your health generally.

ATTAINING BREATHING-MOVEMENT COORDINATION

When breathing keeps pace with muscular effort, that's the *rhythmic flow* that helps your muscles work at peak performance, providing you with a maximum amount of energy. This principle is of supreme importance in your Boutelle natural-action program. Breathing in and out in correct rhythm with natural-actions produces and maintains a smooth flow of power.

Each of your muscles is a source of potential power to operate your body machine at your greatest possible efficiency. Muscle power produces energy, which results in drive. The most important muscle, the heart, is your spark of life—like the battery of your car. If the battery is dead, the car won't function; the same is true if the heart muscle fails. Each muscle, including the heart, is composed of millions of fibers, and the muscle contracts as its fibers are stimulated.

Proper breathing, in coordination with other natural-actions, serves to stimulate and help your heart and all your muscles to perform well, and to provide plenty of energy, drive, and stamina. A student, Dorothy P., told me, "During my husband's emergency surgery after a near-fatal auto accident, I paced the hospital corridor for three hours. The simple natural-actions of breathing in and breathing out rhythmically, deeply and fully, as you taught me, helped keep my energy up and my tension under control."

Are you ready to start learning how to breathe correctly? First, sitting or standing, take a deep breath and then . . .

"BLOW LIKE A WHALE!"

That's right, pursing your lips slightly as though blowing a horn or blowing up a balloon, *blow like a whale* through your mouth. That expression has become an ingrained part of the Boutelle program from the start, so much that I have accumulated a collection of miniature whales over the years, gifts from grateful students. The gift cards usually state, "Thanks for teaching me to *blow like a whale!*"

Each class begins with those words which simply mean exhaling stale air from the lungs by blowing out forcefully. The vital objective is to blow out carbon dioxide from the very bottom of the lungs. Then you take a deep breath through your nose, thus pulling in oxygen and pushing it to the bottom of your lungs, filling the lobes or chambers from bottom to top. The more carbon dioxide you blow out, the more room for energizing oxygen to fill in.

Think of it as filling a container with liquid, from the bottom up, of course. However, due to the lightness of air, you have to breathe in very *deeply* in order to force the air to the bottom of your lungs; shallow breathing won't do it. Most of my students (you, too, very likely) begin as shallow breathers. At the end of the very first class they rush up to tell me that they feel better already. They have enjoyed the uplifting experience that comes from deep breathing and rhythmic flow while moving the muscles. Their lungs have enjoyed it too as they have taken in oxygen and expelled carbon dioxide more efficiently. That is one of the reasons why I call the Boutelle program the *inside-out* way to neuromuscular fitness.

When I took my initial First Aid course years ago, and practiced rhythmic artificial respiration on a volunteer, I was taught to *press down* with my hands and say, "Out goes the bad air," then *release the pressure*, and, "In comes the good air." Think of that as you practice your own rhythmic-flow breathing. Blow like a whale—and "out goes the bad air." Then breathe in deeply through your nose, and "in comes the good air."

As a beginner especially, you need to inhale a large amount of oxygen to help keep your muscles from tiring. To your delight, you will find that gradually, as your muscles gain increased elasticity (*tonus*), they are able to absorb oxygen from inhaled air more proficiently, and you go on and on without tiring.

Blowing like a whale helps to relieve tension as well as gain a new burst of energy. A man in a "His and Her" class told me excitedly, "In yesterday's World Series game, the pitcher was in a tough spot, bases loaded. Before his next pitch I saw him take a deep breath and then *blow like a whale*, just as you taught us. Then he shot the ball over the plate with blinding speed." You, too, will benefit from similar quick tension relief and instant added energy.

PRACTICE RHYTHMIC-FLOW BREATHING NOW

1. Stand with your feet set firmly and comfortably a few inches apart, toes pointing straight forward. (It doesn't matter how you are dressed.) Think IN, think UP, keep pectoral pins IN always while inhaling and exhaling. Raise your arms so that your elbows and wrists are directly over your shoulder caps . . . reach as high as you can . . . let your palms face forward. Now you are ready to . . .

2a. *Blow like a whale* by breathing out through your mouth . . . and as you breathe out, flex your wrists and push your arms *forward and down* s-l-o-w-l-y to your sides, as though forcing the resisting air down, not bending your elbows . . . 2b. and *at the same time*, bend your knees forward a little until they are directly over your toes. In effect, feel yourself *blowing* your arms down as though the act of breathing out is pushing your arms (and knees) down.

3. Now *breathe in* slowly and deeply through your nose as you raise your straight arms in breathing rhythm forward and up, palms facing down and then to front as arms go up . . . and slowly

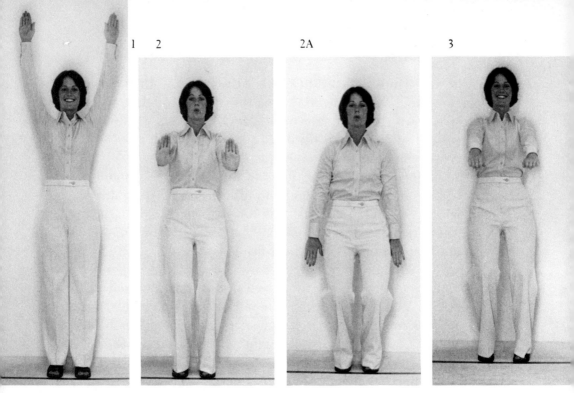

1 2 2A 3

straighten your legs at the same time ... and you are back to start-ing position (as you breathe in, you are getting ready for the next natural-action of breathing out).

Repeat the total exhale-inhale sequence *five times*. You are learn-ing and practicing rhythmic-flow breathing. Notice how you are maintaining and enjoying a new flow of power, without forcing yourself—you are *running smooth*. After all these years, you are finally learning how to breathe most effectively—all part of your new advance to *lifetime fitness through natural-actions*.

TENNIS SWING BREATHING

Now practice rhythmic-flow breathing and movement as though you are swinging a tennis racquet (you don't have to be a tennis player, although this can help improve your game).

1. In the same natural, comfortable standing position, get ready to swing by breathing in deeply through your nose, and *at the same time*, as though holding a racquet, raise your straight right arm (or left, if you are left-handed) to the side so your hand is about the height of your hip socket, and back slightly, in rhythm with your *inhaling* air . . .

2. Follow through by breathing out through your mouth (blow like a whale!) as you swing your straight arm slowly forward and across the front of your body (not bending arm or moving your body) . . . loosely clenched hand lined up with your hip sockets all the way . . . as you exhale in rhythm with your slowly swinging arm. Notice how the action of pushing out breath is helping to swing your arm around with seemingly little muscular exertion. Think IN, think UP throughout the actions.

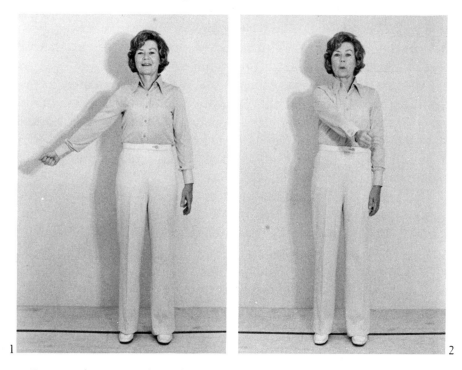

Repeat the in-out breathing and arm-swinging natural-action *five times*, saying to yourself:

Breathe IN—swing back . . .
Breathe OUT—follow through.

CORRECT SLOW BREATHING ESSENTIAL TO YOUR FITNESS

With this *slow*, rhythmic, coordinated breathing-and-movement, your body releases energy far more efficiently than if you were performing these actions in *rapid-fire* succession without matching breathing to actions. Your muscles would soon tire, your energy would be depleted, and you would soon feel exhausted and discouraged. That happens on tennis courts and in other activities daily.

A typical example is Sue R., who was persuaded by friends that she would get a new lease on life by taking up tennis. She bought the most advanced racquet, balls, a smashing outfit, and eagerly went out on the court fully equipped—*outwardly*. But her undertoned skeletal muscles were weak, and her breathing was shallow and haphazard. After running and swinging her racquet for a short time, she began to tire and gasp for air: she was suffering from oxygen depletion and lack of muscle tone. The next day she felt sore all over and moaned, "Tennis is not for me."

I've seen that unhappy sequence many times. Fortunately in this instance, a friend told Sue that her basic poor condition was responsible for her failure. She joined my natural-action program, learned rhythmic-flow breathing, and attained neuromuscular fitness. After a month she went out on the court again—now she is a tennis enthusiast and is developing into a fine player.

This major part of your fitness program is of prime significance to you: The combination of breathing and moving in a rhythmic flow keeps you running smooth, and sustains and improves life whether you are engaged in household chores, office work, or sports. It's no fun when your respiration and combustion are faulty, when you huff and puff, feel sluggish, and living is laborious.

Remember this basic breathing guide, easy to understand when you picture a swimmer blowing OUT as she strokes the water, and inhaling between strokes. Then apply that guide to your daily actions:
• *PULLING movement* (contracting, flexing, bending action)—as in pulling out a tight bureau drawer—equals breathing IN, inhaling air . . .
• *PUSHING movement* (extending and expanding action)—as in pushing the tight drawer shut—equals breathing OUT, blowing out air.

Practice the two breathing natural-actions in this chapter each *five times* in sequence—and often during the day and evening. As that coordinated breathing-and-movement become part of your everyday graceful actions, you will enjoy a wonderful feeling of well-being all over, of new aliveness as you move, walk, work, and function better than ever before.

TEST YOUR BLOWING POWER

Try this simple test, it's fun: Hold your right arm out straight in front of your face, locking the elbow. Now flex your wrist so that the palm of your hand faces you. Take a deep breath through your nose slowly—then B-L-O-W so that you feel your breath against your palm as strongly as possible. Do it *five times*, and as you *inhale*, say to yourself, "IN comes the fresh air" . . . and as you *exhale*, say to yourself, "OUT goes the bad air!"

After a few weeks of your Boutelle program, you'll be thrilled by the greatly improved force of the air on your palm as you learn to "blow like a whale!"

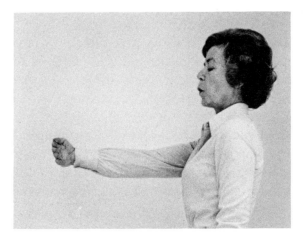

V
Two Quick Neuromuscular Anytime Energizers

To start you building your lifetime fitness at once, here are two quick neuromuscular energizers that you can begin benefiting from and enjoying right now—using your new "blow like a whale" rhythmic-flow breathing technique. (We call them "Q" for "Quick": Q-1 and Q-2). Each natural-action takes only about a minute but picks you up at once. Use these energizers several times a day and evening, at work or rest, any time you may start to sag or just want a quick lift. Like all Boutelle natural-actions, go through these slowly, comfortably, with graceful, flowing movements.

Q-1 SITTING ENERGIZER

Sit on a fairly hard straight chair rather than sinking into a soft upholstered seat. Hold your body straight but never rigid. As always when seated anywhere, sit in correct sitting alignment (Chapter III). Sit way up, supported solidly by your sitting bones, not slouching back on the base of your spine as most people do. Immediately you are automatically thinking UP . . .

1. Place your hands flat across the front of your body, just below your rib cage, so that your middle fingertips touch in the center of

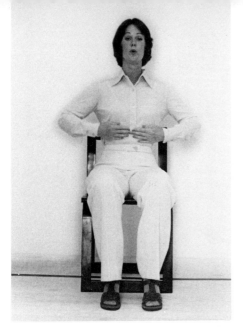

your diaphragm. Take a really deep breath in slowly through your nose . . . and as you breathe in, think IN, and press your flat palms and fingers gently but firmly against your diaphragm, *pushing in.* (Realize that you are combining think IN and think UP . . . your breathing action is lifting your diaphragm, as you feel with your hands, and you are lifting your rib cage UP.)

2. With lungs filled, breathe out slowly (blow like a whale!), while relaxing your hands but keeping them in place on your diaphragm, and keeping your rib cage up.

Repeat this one-two natural-action energizer *five times.* This process fills your lungs to their greatest present capacity (which will increase as you proceed week after week with your entire program). It serves to activate and improve your respiratory system and vital lung capacity.

You will feel a helpful energizing *lift* every time you perform this quick neuromuscular energizer. It helps relieve tension, clear your head, brighten your eyes—the little pickup we all need at least a few times through the day, whether working hard or at leisure.

Q-2 STANDING ENERGIZER

Stand erect in correct standing alignment (Chapter III) . . . straight but comfortable, not stiff as a board, not slumping or sagging . . . arms at sides, palms facing in . . .

1. *Breathe in deeply* through your nose as you raise your straight arms, palms facing up, in an arc out at your sides and up high over

1   2

your head, completing the circle . . . arms straight up in alignment with your shoulder sockets. (Feel your diaphragm contract during this natural-action as you think IN and think UP . . . note how filling your lungs with air helps lift your arms smoothly.)

2. Now *breathe out* through your mouth (blow like a whale!) as you return your straight arms, palms facing down, gracefully and rhythmically in an arc to your sides, to original starting position.

Repeat total one-two action *five times*, feeling the rhythmic flow of breathing and movement, running smooth.

Do you feel nicely reenergized? You should if you went through these two easy natural-actions correctly. Understand that these quick energizers are just a little extra part of your neuromuscular conditioning, to be used as you see fit any time of day, almost anywhere, as an adjunct to your entire program. No matter how busy you are, you can and should afford the minute or so for both energizers at least a few times each day, suited to your personal convenience and mood.

VI

Three Self-Tests
to Check Your Fitness
Before You Begin

Before you start your daily program, check some basic facets of your condition right now, with three simple self-tests related directly to three fundamental Boutelle goals.

TEST ONE: CORRECT BODY ALIGNMENT

This is a double test that may seem too easy for you at first thought. However, you cannot achieve your top personal all-over neuromuscular fitness unless you attain the objective of realigning your body properly so that you function most smoothly and safely in all your movements. Pick a spot in front of a full-size mirror. Wear whatever you wish for these tests, but preferably not a dress or other garment that conceals the full lengths of your arms and legs for your opening test.

First, stand the way you normally do, facing the mirror. What does your reflection reveal? Like most people, are you out of alignment? Check "yes" or "no" on the following listing:

	YES	NO	
1.	____	____	Is your head tilting a little forward or backward instead of up comfortably, chin and neck relaxed?
2.	____	____	Shoulders rounded or slumped rather than up, aligned with your trunk, pectoral pins IN?
3.	____	____	Chest caved in rather than held high from the uplifting action of thinking UP, standing Tall?
4.	____	____	Abdomen mushily "hanging" out instead of pulled IN toward your spine by thinking IN?
5.	____	____	Knees slightly bent and unsure rather than locked to keep legs straight and supportive?
6.	____	____	Ankles and feet very close, even tight together, instead of ankle joints directly under hip sockets, feet a few inches apart for natural, firm support?

Please fix in your retentive mind's eye that image of the way you stand normally as reflected by your mirror right now . . .

Next, reread "Standing in Correct Alignment" (Chapter III), study the photograph and take that position as instructed. See the enormous improvement at once in the way you look, in the more attractive trimness of your figure, and in the comfort and aliveness of standing proudly and comfortably in correct alignment.

For the second part of this body alignment test, set a straight chair in front of the mirror. Seat yourself as you would normally, not the way you think you should sit (there is no benefit in fooling yourself). Again, examine your normal posture and answer the same yes-no questions, omitting number 5, in respect to your sitting appearance.

I have been repeatedly appalled to note the ungainly and damaging slouches and slumps of people sitting in a room, an office, riding a bus—droopily collapsed in loose lumps and bumps like a half-empty sack of potatoes dumped on the seat. No wonder so many people complain of assorted aches and pains, and groan, "Oh, my aching back!"

Now reread "Sitting in Correct Alignment" (Chapter III), study the photo, and follow the instructions for sitting up healthfully and supportively. See the remarkable improvement in your figure, and enjoy the way your body feels firmer inside and out—alive, taller, astonishingly more attractive.

Most people, being honest with themselves, fail in these tests, scoring practically all "yesses" on each test. How did you score? Even if your total is as many as five or six "Yesses," amounting in effect to *zero*—I assure you that you can definitely change all that with the Boutelle Method to a *perfect* score in a short time. In fact, you reflect improved standing and sitting alignment immediately, and increasingly thereafter.

Repeat this double test two weeks after you have started your "A" or "M" program—and then a month later. The ungainly "before" slumping standing and sitting body that you viewed at the start of the test will be replaced by a trimmer, far more attractive figure and posture. You will answer people proudly when they ask, "You look wonderful—what have you been doing for yourself? Found a marvelous new diet or super-vitamins? Been on vacation?"

The "marvelous" thing that will have happened for you is that your body will be trimmer and more attractive not only because you are more fit all over—but also because correct, more healthful alignment standing, sitting, and moving will have become a natural part of your daily actions.

TEST TWO: NEUROMUSCULAR TONING AND COORDINATION

This second self-test is an important checkup of your neuromuscular fitness, coordination, and balance. It is based on a common action you probably perform many times a day—picking up something from the floor, or opening a bottom bureau drawer, or plugging a vacuum cleaner or lamp or other item into a baseboard socket. Just learning this simple natural-action, and making it your bending-down method from now on, will be worth many times more than the cost of this book in averting pain, suffering, and medical bills.

Bend down now in your usual way (be careful!) to pick up an invisible scrap of paper from the floor. Check how you did it:

YES   NO

1. ___ ___ Did you stand stiff-legged and bend down from the hips?
2. ___ ___ Did you bend both knees slightly and round your back way over to pick up the scrap?
3. ___ ___ With feet close together, did you unlock both knees in a deep knee bend as you reached for the scrap?

If you answered "yes" to any one of these questions, as most people do, you are risking back and neck injury, as well as feeling uncoordinated and unbalanced every time you bend down. You will learn how to bend down properly when you get to Chapter X and read what I call the "Dustpan-and-Brush" natural-action in my classes.

TEST THREE: NEUROMUSCULAR ENDURANCE

As noted in Chapter IV, improving your respiratory system through rhythmic flow deep breathing is a vital part of building *stamina* so that you can move through active days, sports, any activities, without becoming breathless and exhausted. A basic necessity for endurance is the correct coordinating of breathing and body movements. If you are like most people, you are probably way below your top functional ability in this area, with below-par *vital lung capacity*. That will be improved within a relatively short time through your daily Boutelle program.

Right now, test yourself by trying Tennis Swing Breathing again (Chapter IV). Do it slowly as in the simple directions—no more than three times at most for the test. You will probably find yourself somewhat awkward at this point, having some difficulty in coordinating breathing and action in a rhythmic flow. However, test yourself again with Tennis Swing Breathing after two weeks in your daily program. You will discover that doing Tennis Swing Breathing—as well as breathing with all daily actions and Boutelle natural-actions—has become truly smooth, natural and enjoyable.

Doing the coordinated breathing/movement natural-action two weeks from now—five times and more in slow, smooth rhythm—should be a cinch for you. In following months, you will find that much of your previous daily fatigue, even exhaustion, have dissipated—and that your endurance has improved remarkably, as it will continue to do week after week from now on.

Repeat all three tests every few weeks as you advance—and the results will provide you with gratifying proof of your greater all-over fitness.

VII

Your Daily Ten-Minute "A" Alpha Program

The Boutelle "A" Alpha Program is the beginning of your daily sessions for new and enduring lifetime fitness through *natural-actions*. No matter how good an "athlete" you have been up to now, or how inactive, you need this all-over, inside-out neuromuscular body conditioning.

I have selected all the "A" natural-actions with *safety* as one basic factor, to avoid any possible overstraining and injury, as you follow directions carefully. You will be using and conditioning all 632 muscles in this program, aligning and firming your body all over. You will be building vigor and stamina for your total better functioning in all phases of everyday and sports activity.

Determine that your daily session is not just something you "ought" to do, but *must* do for your maximum good health, energy, endurance, and total well-being. Inform everyone that you need this brief private time every day. Turn off the telephone; don't permit any interruptions except for a real emergency.

I can't repeat this too often: If you feel at all strained, breathless, quivery—STOP. After resting, start again if you feel fine. Halt at any slightest discomfort (none should occur with Boutelle natural-actions done correctly). Tomorrow is another day to begin once more and to improve steadily and surely. You will be thrilled by your increasing grace, energy and well-being day after day and week after week.

Special Note: If you have a particular medical problem, such as a bad back or other impairment, start with the "M" Medical Referral Program, Chapter IX, not the "A" program (you will probably advance to that stage later). In any case, remember that you are to get your doctor's approval before starting the Boutelle Method or any other activity program (show your physician this book).

S-M-I-L-E . . . fitness should be fun! You will be starting the day *bright* with your enjoyable Boutelle session. And you will find that moving your body in smooth, flowing rhythms with natural-actions is so pleasurable, the ten minutes are over before you know it. You'll feel so good that you'll look forward to each session.

Enjoy music as you move. Many Boutelle enthusiasts say that they get extra pleasure when they turn on the radio and tune to a music station, and move to the rhythm of music; others move to the beat of music cassettes. Still others prefer it quiet—it's up to you to do your own thing in your own way.

In performing Boutelle natural-actions, it's preferable that you wear loose clothing, a leotard if you wish, shirts and shorts—or nothing—just so you feel comfortable. Many start the day with an A session in pajamas, a perfect beginning for a *better* day.

Lie on a carpeted or other floor surface, wherever you have enough space and find it convenient.

BASIC POSITION "A" FOR YOUR ALPHA PROGRAM

The first four "A" natural-actions begin on your back, with your body in repose, head at rest, in the following comfortable position: Relax your head against the floor. Keep your shoulders firmly against the floor in a holding pattern throughout the series, your invisible "pushpins" pinning each shoulder to the floor. Pull your tummy in to help keep your entire back against the floor from shoulders through pelvis.

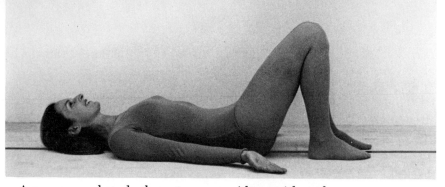

Arms are relaxed close to your sides, with palms up . . . upper arms tucked close to your body like a sheet on a bed.

Flex your knees, keeping your knee joints aligned with your hip sockets. Place your lower legs as close to your hip sockets as comfortable for you with feet flat on the floor . . . feet a few inches apart, not close together, so that your ankles line up with your hip sockets and knees.

Maintain this basic alignment throughout the program. Your total body alignment, grace, and balance while standing, sitting, walking will improve naturally, beautifully.

To relax completely before starting, breathe in through your nose deeply and slowly (lying in basic position A) . . . then expel breath through your mouth (*blow like a whale!*). *Repeat three times.*

A-1 THE CINCH

This simple, excellent natural-action strengthens leg muscles and pelvic girdle (midriff area) muscles, flattening and firming your abdomen, waist, hips, buttocks. It is named "The Cinch" from the verb "to gird or bind firmly," which this does wonderfully.

1. Lie in basic position A, but with feet pointed down, toes touching floor. Keep feet a few inches apart in alignment with hip sockets.

2. *Inhale* as you bring both legs back, knees flexed . . . flex ankles so toes point toward ceiling . . . bringing upper legs back as close to your abdomen as possible without straining.

3. *Blow out* as you return slowly to position (1), pointing toes until they touch the floor again. *Important:* Keep your back firmly against the floor throughout; if your back and abdominal muscles start to lift before your toes touch the floor, *immediately* flex your ankles so that toes point up toward ceiling, and bring upper legs back to your chest again as you *inhale*.

Repeat lifting-lowering action slowly, rhythmically, *five times*.

Self-checks: (a) The first time your toes touch the floor (3), try to push your hand under the small of your back; there shouldn't be space for your hand since your back should be snug against the floor. (b) The second time you lower your toes to the floor (3), place a hand flat against your abdomen where muscles should be flattening out; if your abdominal muscles begin to lift, immediately start your toes and lower legs back slowly to knees-to-chest position. Soon you'll find that your entire back stays flat against the floor, and your tightened abdominal muscles pull down instead of lifting up—a great advance.

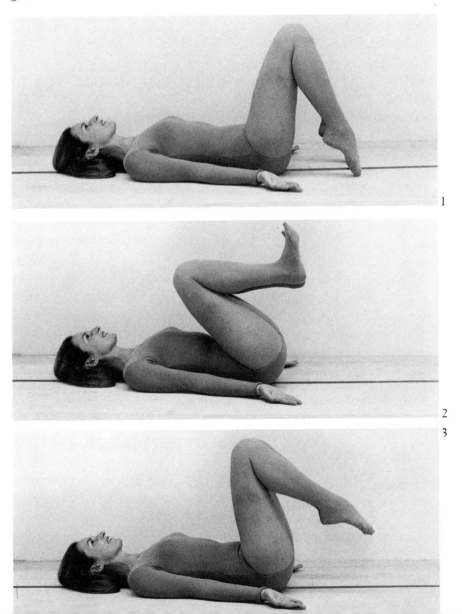

A-2 PEDAL STRETCH FORWARD

This natural-action strengthens your pelvic girdle area and promotes and increases the smooth, enduring mobility of your ankles, knees, and hip sockets. Lie in basic position A, knees flexed, feet flat against floor . . .

1. *Inhale* . . . then *exhale* vigorously (blow!) as you stretch your right leg in a straight line forward fully, flexing your ankle so that your toes now point toward the ceiling—as though you are reaching forward firmly to press a pedal that is an inch above the floor . . .

2. *Inhale* as you pull your right knee back toward your shoulder, pointing your toes forward. Do all actions slowly, exerting effort but without straining . . .

3. *Exhale* as you return right leg to starting position . . . touching floor first with your toes, then bringing your heel down so foot is flat on floor.

Alternate this right leg action with similar left leg action slowly. *five times each leg*, for total of ten times.

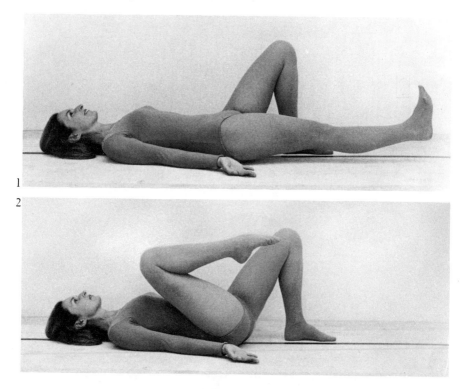

A-3 PEDAL STRETCH UPWARD

This is designed to improve muscle tone (firmness, flexibility, elasticity) in legs, strengthen pelvic girdle muscles, and promote mobility of ankle, knee, and hip joints. Lie in basic position A, knees flexed, feet flat on floor . . .

1. *Inhale* deeply as you pull your right knee back toward your shoulder, pointing your toes forward. (Again, do all movements slowly, exerting effort but never straining.)

2. *Exhale* as you stretch your right leg up toward the ceiling, flexing your ankle as though to press your foot flat against a pedal fixed in the ceiling. Extend your right leg up as straight as possible, keeping ankle aligned with your hip socket. Then, flexing your right knee, return knee toward your shoulder, toes pointed forward . . . *inhaling*.

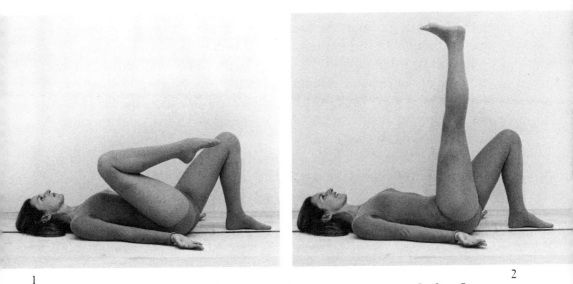

1　　　　　　　　　　　　　　　　　　　　　　　　　　2

3. *Exhale* as you push your right foot back toward the floor, pointing your toes as you bring foot downward, touching toes to floor, then lowering heel until your foot is flat against the floor.

Alternate right leg action with similar left leg action *five times with each leg* for a total of *ten times*. Your legs will straighten upward more and more readily as you repeat this excellent limbering-flexing natural-action daily.

A-4 BOUTELLE NO-STRAIN PELVIC TILT

Different from many types of so-called "pelvic tilts," which have been adapted by others from my original creation, this natural-

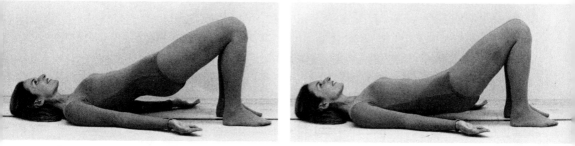

1   2

action strengthens your pelvic muscles and particularly the *internal muscles of the lower digestive tract*, vital to your improved functioning—*without strain*.

Lie in basic position A. Keep inhaling and exhaling slowly and deeply throughout this natural-action, never holding your breath.

1. Roll your buttocks and lower spine up s-l-o-w-l-y, starting from the base of your spinal column (coccyx) . . . rolling up gradually to the middle of your back, just below where a bra strap hooks. (Anatomically, you are rolling up slowly over ten lumbar and thoracic vertebrae—superb conditioning.)

2. Lower to your original position to a slow count of ten, rolling down on your vertebrae one by one.

Important: Keep your abdominal muscles pulled in (think IN!) throughout. Keep your head, neck and shoulders relaxed but in a firm holding pattern, not rounding or hunching.

Repeat total action five times, benefiting and gaining new strength and midriff flatness from the s-l-o-w rolling motions.

A-5 STRETCH-FLEX COORDINATOR

You gain three primary triple-benefits from this energizing natural-action: it (a) strengthens your pelvic muscles; (b) tones flexor and extensor leg muscles; and (c) coordinates mobility of ankle, knee, and hip sockets working in unison.

1. *Inhale* . . . lie relaxed on back, arms at sides, palms up. *Exhale* as you flex knees and bring legs up so that right knee is over right

hip, left knee over left hip . . . lower legs at right angles to upper legs, parallel to floor. Flex ankles so toes point straight up . . .

2. Now *inhale* deeply . . . then *blow out* slowly as you push your lower legs upward toward the ceiling so ankles are directly over respective hip joints . . . soles of feet parallel to ceiling . . .

3. *Inhale* deeply as you stretch legs up fully and point toes to ceiling . . .

4. *Exhale*, keeping toes pointed, and flex knees to bring lower legs back to starting position, but with toes pointed . . .

5. As you *inhale*, flex ankles back to starting position with toes pointed upward toward ceiling.

Repeat this five-part stretching-flexing action *five times*.

1

2

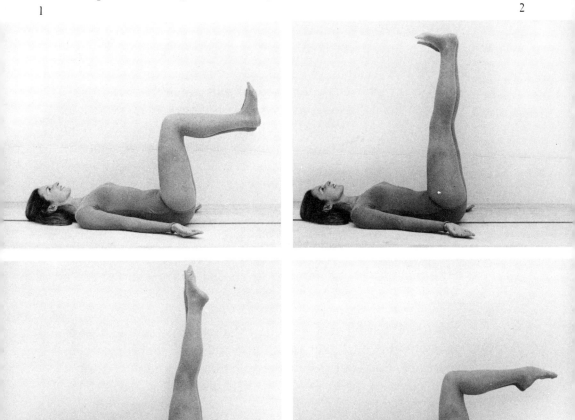

3

4

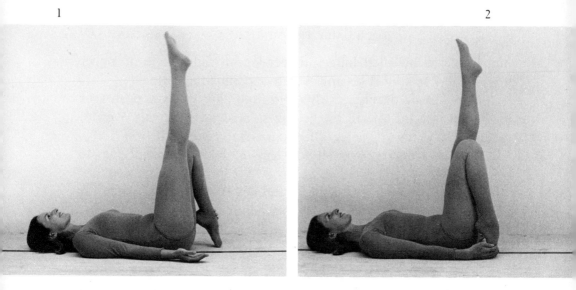

A-6 SHIFTING GEARS

While strengthening and toning your pelvic and leg muscles, you will improve the flexibility of your knee joints by shifting your knee hinges through their maximum range of movement. *Important:* Always do knee flexing gently; never snap up your legs or overstrain your knees—they are the most complicated joints in the body, and must be treated respectfully. Strenuous "exercises" that call for straining and snapping up the knee joints can be very harmful.

1. Lie on your back . . . arms close against sides . . . palms up. *Inhale* deeply. Extend your *right* leg in the air as straight up as possible without straining . . . knee hinge extended and locked . . . ankle aligned over right hip joint . . . toes pointed up. Flex your *left* knee fully . . . pointed toes touching floor as close as you can to your left hip joint without straining (if needed, grasp your left ankle with your left hand and pull gently to help your toes touch the floor).

2. Now start shifting, inhaling and exhaling slowly throughout to your own rhythm. Flex your right knee and bring right leg down, toes pointed, so that your right toes touch floor in front of your right hip socket (grasping right ankle with right hand if needed). *At the same time*, straighten up your left leg . . . lock knee in position . . . toes pointed toward ceiling. Alternate right and left leg positions slowly, rhythmically *ten times*.

Don't be concerned if you are a little awkward at first; you'll be "shifting gears" smoothly and gracefully in a week or so.

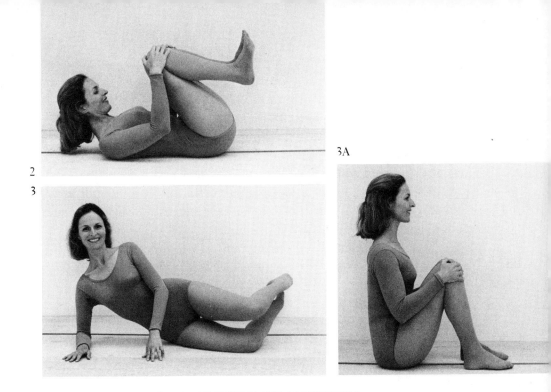

A-6 to A-7 LYING-TO-SITTING TRANSITION

To avoid any back strain and awkwardness, here's how I want you to learn to *flow* from A-6, on your back, to the A-7 sitting position—and any time you go from lying to sitting . . .

1. Lie in basic position A (page 64) . . .

2. *Inhale* as you pull your knees up over your chest, hands gripping just below knees, which are aligned a few inches apart. Lift head to tuck chin on your chest, and look through your separated knees . . . don't strain . . .

3. *Exhale* as you lift your left hip and roll to your right, pushing up with your left hand on floor about ten inches in front of your chest, your right hand supportively against the floor . . . in the same fluid motion, roll your body up gracefully into sitting position for A-7, hands pulling your knees up to your chest.

Practice this lying-to-sitting transition a few times, and it will become a natural part of your graceful, no-strain actions.

A-7 GENTLE NECK STRETCH

Knowing and respecting the natural anatomy thoroughly, I warn strongly against strenuous neck "exercises" often offered. This careful, free-flowing movement provides primary double benefits (a) to activate and improve pivotal motions of the neck, and (b) to maintain back and shoulder muscles in correct alignment. *Gentle moderation* is your guide in doing this superb natural-action.

1. *Inhale* as you sit on the floor with back and neck aligned straight up. Flex your knees so that your feet rest flat on the floor a few inches apart, each ankle aligned with the corresponding hip socket. Clasp knees with your hands, keeping elbows tucked close to your sides throughout.

2. Keep your eyes closed during this relaxing, restorative natural-action. *Exhale* as you lower head s-l-o-w-l-y so that your chin touches your chest.

3. Slowly *inhale* as you lift your head and flex your neck back so that your eyes would look up at the ceiling. Repeat forward-back-forward action slowly *five times*, keeping shoulders firmly in place and spine in straight alignment throughout.

4. In same sitting position, *inhaling* deeply, lower your chin to your chest, and rotate your head slowly so that you are looking over your *right* shoulder . . .

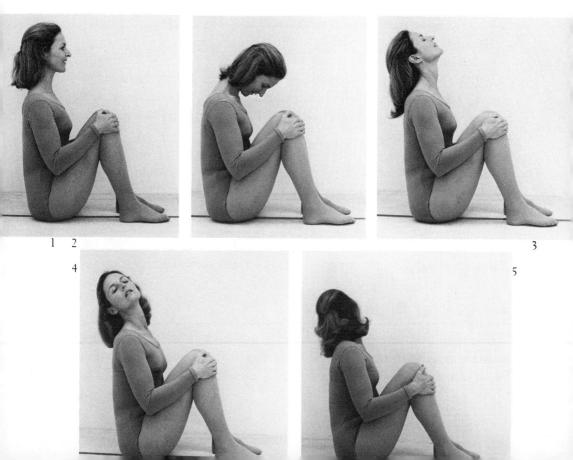

1   2   3

4   5

5. *Exhale* as you swivel your head back slowly from right to left, so that your chin describes a half-circle on your chest, and now you are looking over your *left* shoulder . . .

Now swivel slowly from left to right . . . back from right to left . . . alternating inhaling and exhaling . . . until you complete *five half-circles in each direction*.

Caution: All actions must be very slow—never the slightest straining, snapping, or jerking of head or neck, which can be damaging.

A-8 ROWING ACTION

This enjoyable all-over conditioner strengthens leg, arm and pelvic muscles, while maintaining back and shoulder girdle muscles in firming alignment. For maximum neuromuscular benefits, keep head up, shoulders in comfortable, unmoving "holding pattern," back straight, no slumping. Think IN, think UP through all actions.

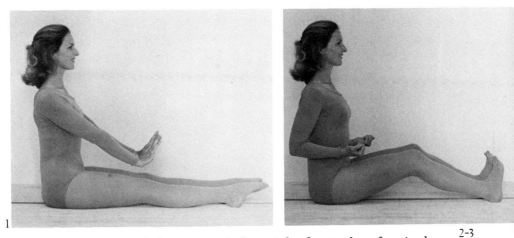

1. Sit on floor with legs extended straight forward, a few inches apart, with ankles and hips in alignment, toes pointed forward . . . back straight . . . straight arms extended forward and downward so hands are close to but not touching knee joints . . . wrists flexed with fingers spread up as though to push a weight forward . . .

2. *Inhale* as you slowly flex knees and ankles so that only heels remain on floor (don't let heels slide forward or backward) . . . toes slowly pointing upward . . . and 3. *at the same time*, make hands into fists . . . and in continuing movement, flex elbows and wrists,

thus bringing palm sides of fists back close to hip sockets, *as though pulling on oars* (keep elbows close to sides of body!).

4. *Exhale* as you return arms, hands and legs to starting position 1. Repeat entire rowing actions rhythmically *ten times*.

A-9 THE WAVE

This superb spine conditioner flexes and extends the spinal cord and supporting spinal muscles as it firms the midriff.

1. Sit on floor with legs extended fully, ankles in alignment with hip sockets, toes pointed forward . . . spine held straight and head erect . . . hands over shoulder caps, arms aligned with sides of chest, and elbows out two or three inches from sides (be careful not to lift shoulders). *Inhale* deeply . . .

2. Keeping shoulders in firm holding position, pectoral pins in place, *exhale* as you bend forward to tuck chin on chest . . . roll trunk forward slowly and bring elbows against front of hip sockets . . . move rolled trunk further forward so that elbows describe straight lines over thighs, and elbows almost sit on kneecaps . . .

3. *Inhale* as you unroll trunk and head slowly, bringing elbows back to starting position . . . then stretch out elbows at sides, still holding shoulder caps, so your upper arms go straight out at sides at

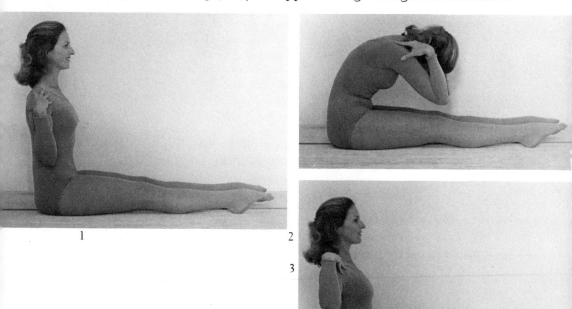

1

2

3

shoulder height. Bring elbows back down to starting position at sides.

Repeat actions 2 and 3 slowly *five times*.

Important: Keep legs extended and firm against floor without lifting or flexing knees, rolling trunk forward only as far as you can *without straining*. Within a week, you will easily be able to roll your trunk much further forward while keeping legs firm against floor.

A-9 to A-10   ALL-FOURS SAFETY TRANSITION

Instead of moving awkwardly and with possible strain from sitting on the floor with legs stretched out for A-9, to all fours for A-10, here's your graceful safety roll-over . . .

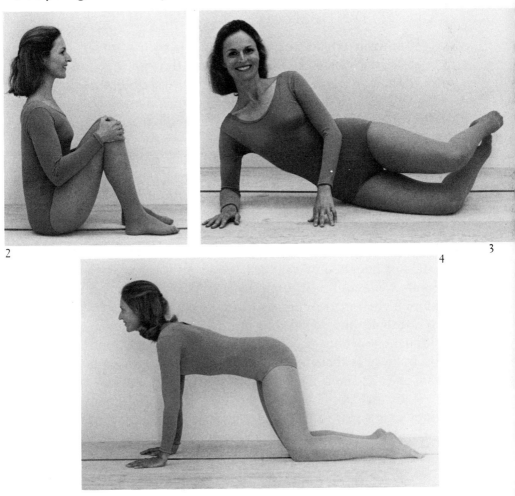

2

4

3

1. Sit in A-9 starting position, legs stretched out on floor . . .

2. *Inhale* as you pull your knees up to your chest, hands gripping just below knees, which are aligned a few inches apart . . .

3. *Exhale* as you lift your left hip and roll over to your right, supporting the action by bringing your left hand and then right hand down on floor in natural pushing-up placement . . . rolling over on your left knee and then right knee in natural sequence . . .

4. Straighten your arms so that your body lifts easily into all-fours position to begin A-10 . . . body aligned solidly and comfortably, arms and knees a few inches apart. Check to make sure your wrists are directly under arm sockets, knees under hip sockets.

You'll enjoy practicing this fluid action and mastering it quickly.

A-10   KITTEN CURL

This highly effective natural-action has been a top favorite among thousands of women in Boutelle classes through the years. Graceful and fun, it is the first natural-action you will do based on the basic Boutelle all-fours position, which (a) strengthens pelvic girdle muscles while relaxing tension in shoulder girdle muscles; (b) establishes correct spinal alignment and strengthens muscles supporting the spine; and (c) eases tensions in the cervical spine.

1. Place yourself on floor on all fours with arms extended, elbows locked . . . hands flat on floor . . . wrists directly under shoulder joints . . . knees flexed, upper legs at right angles to floor, lower legs on floor apart . . . toes pointed back . . . knee joints aligned under hip sockets. Back flat, not rounded—keep shoulders firm throughout, not hunched or slumped. Head up as you face forward. Feel comfortable and well supported, with hands and feet about six or more inches apart in proper hip-knee, shoulder-wrist alignment . . .

2. Inhale and exhale deeply and slowly in your own rhythm throughout actions. Keeping elbows locked, push your body directly back slowly as though someone is pulling on a rope attached to your tailbone . . . move back as far as possible without any straining . . .

3. In that position, flex your elbows and roll body down slowly until your forearms, wrists and hands are flat against the floor. Keep elbows in so that wrist, elbow, knee and ankle joints stay in alignment . . .

1   2-3

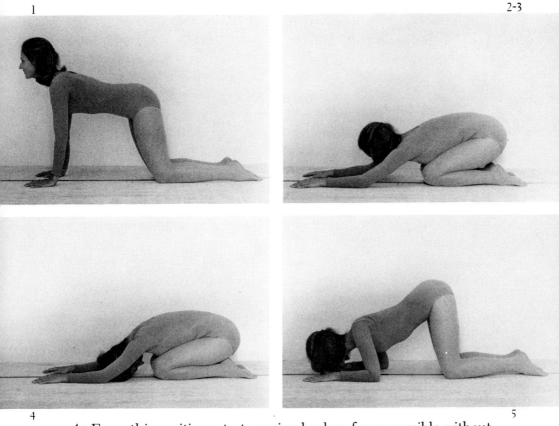

4   5

4. From this position, start moving back as far as possible without any straining, aiming your tailbone again toward your heels . . . while curling your head forward so your chin rests on your chest, and you are looking back between your heels (your elbows are still flexed, with elbows, forearms, and hands still flat against the floor) . . .

5. Now slowly roll your head and body forward, keeping your face close to the floor as though pushing a peanut with your nose, until your nose is even with your thumbs . . . forearms against the floor . . . keeping your back, shoulders and neck in straight forward alignment, shoulders relaxed . . . as you slowly lift your body and straighten out arms until you are back in starting position 1, on all fours.

Repeat the Kitten Curl slowly six times. You will feel wonderfully conditioned throughout your midsection and back, and without strain.

A-11 OUTREACH

This natural-action conditions and strengthens more of your muscles and tones the lateral muscles of your legs, particularly firming *insides of thighs*. Start in the basic Boutelle all-fours position, as in A-10. *Inhale* deeply . . .

1. *Exhale* as you stretch your *left* leg back in a straight line with your left hip socket, locking knee and resting leg on the ball of your left foot (right leg stays in position) . . .

2. Keeping knee locked and leg straight, stretch your left leg out to the side in line with your right knee, without straining . . . left leg resting on left heel, with toes turned upward . . .

3. Return to position 1 with left leg stretched back . . . then back to all-fours starting position.

Repeat this natural-action *four times* with your left leg . . . then *four times* with your right leg (left knee remaining on floor). Inhale and exhale deeply to your own rhythm after the specified start. You will note that your inside thigh muscles are becoming firmer and that you are much more limber after a week or so of repeating the Boutelle Outreach along with the other natural-actions.

A-12 BOUNCE-STRETCH

This body wake-up action is fun to do, and it flexes your knee joints as well and strengthens your lower back, leg, foot, and pelvic girdle muscles. Start in the basic Boutelle all-fours position (A-10) . . .

1. Bring up your flexed *left* knee so that knee and wrist joints are in line with your ankle and under your shoulder socket. Your straight arms with hands turned to outside are supportive, but your weight rests primarily on left foot which is flat on the floor . . . as

you stretch out your *right* leg straight backwards, right knee locked, resting leg lightly on ball of your right foot . . . your back making a straight line from heel to top of your head . . .

2. Now start *bouncing* your body by flexing your left knee and ankle . . . arms straight . . . body weight supported primarily by left foot and hands flat on floor, and balanced by ball of right foot . . . keeping your right knee locked so leg is straight out in back. *Inhale-exhale* quickly with each rapid body bounce, whistling sharply with each exhalation. Bounce *ten times* in this position.

3. Now reverse legs so that your *left* leg is stretched out straight back, and *right* knee flexes. Bounce *ten times* in this position, and "whistle while you work" with each sharp exhalation.

AFTER YOUR "A" ALPHA PROGRAM

You will feel exhilarated, pepped up, and better conditioned physically and emotionally after each eight- to ten-minute "A" program session.

Continue the Alpha sessions daily (upon arising or other selected convenient time for you)—*for at least four weeks*. Then test yourself with the Three Self-Tests in Chapter VI, and see how vastly your physique and ability have improved since you first tried these tests weeks ago.

If you now perform the three test natural-actions and all the others in the Alpha Program easily and enjoyably, without the slightest strain or difficulty, you are ready to move on to the "B" Best Program. You will be moving on to a more advanced stage of all-over, inside-out, neuromuscular conditioning. Congratulations—and away you go to the next lifetime fitness level . . .

Important: If you still don't feel that you perform the "A" sessions with total ease and mastery, please continue on the Alpha Program, testing yourself again at the end of each week until you are *certain* that you are ready to move to the "B" Program. Your aim is to gain lifetime fitness *within your personal capacities;* you are not trying to win a competition or contest. You will be conditioning your body all over excellently even if you stay with the daily Alpha Program from now on.

EXTRA SESSION: THREE-MINUTE ANYTIME ALL-OVER CONDITIONER

Your daily "A" or "B" (Chapter VIII) program will take you about ten minutes. Many women have asked me for an additional brief session to limber and pep them up all over at any time of the day or evening if they feel pooped or tense. I created for them, and for you, this compact, very enjoyable and effective three-minute mini-session, which works wonders in helping you to feel refreshed and free of strain swiftly. You simply perform one of the quickie energizers plus three of my favorite natural-actions, which are part of your "A" program:

1. Q-2   Standing Energizer (Chapter V)
2. A-1   The Cinch
3. A-4   Boutelle No-Strain Pelvic Tilt
4. A-10   Kitten Curl

VIII
Your Daily Ten-Minute "B" Best Program

Having completed at least four weeks on the "A" Alpha program, and tested yourself to be sure that you perform all the natural-actions without strain, you are ready to go on to the more advanced "B" Best program. (Of course you have your doctor's approval, as stressed earlier.)

You will find the "B" actions fun to do as you soon master them, with your much improved muscle tone, alignment, coordination, and endurance. You will discover smoother, more pliant movement of many of your 632 muscles, such as your leg muscles, which help strengthen your heart and other muscles in turn. Famed heart specialist, Dr. Paul Dudley White, noted that "good muscular tone in the legs helps your heart. It's part of the circulation."

As always, proceed with your "B" program carefully; if you feel any excess stress, strain, shortness of breath, or any other undesirable symptoms: STOP. Go on again after a rest, and develop advanced "B" conditioning gradually, improving your neuromuscular fitness all over.

B-1   BOUTELLE NO-STRAIN PELVIC TILT "B"

This is an added, advanced action to the pelvic tilt you have been doing in the "A" program. It adds further development in firming upper arms and strengthening arm muscles, counteracting flabbiness. Start in basic position A (read page 68 again) . . .

1. Lie on your back, knees flexed, bringing feet as close to hips as you can without straining . . . legs a few inches apart so that ankle joints are aligned with hip sockets. Keep arms as close to sides as possible without touching, hands relaxed with palms facing up. Breathe in deeply . . .

2. Blowing out air strongly, lift straight arms slowly and flex wrists so that palms *push up* as though lifting something heavy . . . move arms upward until wrists are directly over respective hip sockets. Then inhale deeply as you lower straight arms slowly and release wrists, bringing hands back to original position, palms and fingers relaxed facing upward. Repeat action slowly *five times*.

3. Now perform the A-4 Pelvic Tilt . . . and *at same time* repeat lifting straight arms and hands (action 2, above) . . . synchronizing

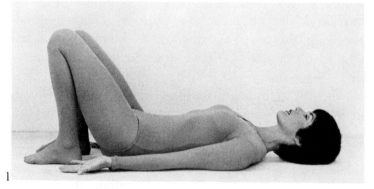

1

2-3

actions so your straight arms lift upward as you roll up your lower spine . . . then lower arms slowly as you roll your body back to starting position . . . always keeping shoulders against floor.

S-l-o-w-l-y perform the coordinated actions *five times*. You will feel the superb conditioning effected in your arms, wrists, and midriff particularly.

B-2   UPBEAT STRETCH-FLEX COORDINATOR

This is the same as Natural-Action A-5 (Chapter VII) but speeded up so that instead of doing *five* repeats, you do *ten* repeats in about the same length of time—in the smooth, effortless rhythm of which you are capable now.

Start in basic position "A" . . .

1. Inhale . . . lie relaxed on back, arms at sides, palms up. Exhale as you flex knees and bring legs up so that right knee is over right hip . . . left knee over left hip . . . lower legs at right angle to upper legs, parallel to floor. Flex ankles so toes point straight up . . .

2. Now inhale deeply . . . then blow out slowly as you push your lower legs upward toward the ceiling so ankles are directly over respective hip joints . . . soles of feet parallel to ceiling . . .

3. Inhale deeply as you stretch legs up fully and point toes to ceiling.

4. Exhale, keeping toes pointed, and flex knees to bring lower legs back to starting position but with toes pointed forward away from your body . . .

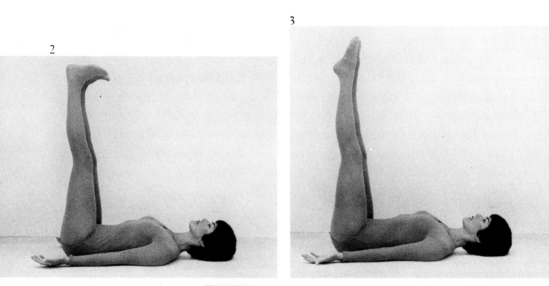

5. As you inhale, flex ankles back to position (1) with toes pointed upward toward ceiling.

Repeat this five-part stretching-flexing action *ten times* in speeded-up action, but not so fast that you become breathless; find your own comfortable, rhythmic, speedy pace.

B-3 UPBEAT SHIFTING GEARS

This is Natural-Action A-5 (Chapter VII) which you will speed up so that instead of *ten* repeats, do *fifteen* repeats in about the same length of time. Remember that you always do knee-flexing gently, never snapping up the leg and knee or overstraining the knees. If you find yourself straining to do fifteen repeats speedily and smoothly, do as many as you can readily, then work up gradually week by week to the full fifteen repeats.

1. Inhale deeply. Lie on your back . . . arms close against sides
. . . palms up. Extend your *right* leg in the air as straight up as
possible without straining . . . knee hinge extended and locked . . .
ankle aligned over right hip joint . . . toes pointed up. Flex your *left*
knee fully . . . pointed toes touching floor as close as you can to
your left hip joint without straining (if needed, grasp your left ankle
with your left hand and pull gently to help your toes touch the
floor).

1   2

2. Now start shifting, inhaling and exhaling slowly throughout to
your own rhythm. Flex your right knee and bring right leg down,
toes pointed . . . so that your right toes touch floor in front of your
right hip socket (grasping right ankle with right hand if needed). *At
the same time*, straighten up your left leg . . . lock knee in position
. . . toes pointed toward ceiling. Alternate right and left leg positions slowly, rhythmically *fifteen times*.

B-4 STRIDE-IN-AIR

This natural-action tones and firms muscles on the inside and
outside of *thighs and lower legs* . . . and rotates the hip sockets for
better body mobility and balance; it is also excellent for relaxing and
aligning shoulders for better posture and endurance. Start in B-1
position . . .

1. Lie flat on your back, arms close to sides, palms up, shoulders

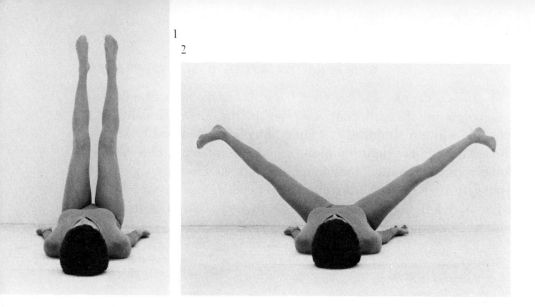

relaxed against floor. *Inhale* as you raise both legs as straight in the air as you can at right angles to your body . . . knees locked . . . toes pointed toward ceiling. Keep legs apart a few inches so that ankles align with hip sockets . . .

2. *Exhale* as you flex ankles and rotate legs from hip sockets so toes point outward . . . spread toes wide, feet still pointed upward . . . and spread legs apart as far as you can without straining. *Inhale* and bring legs back to position straight up in the air, closing toes and rolling feet back to point straight up at ceiling again. Always keep legs in line with hip sockets at right angles to body—*don't let your legs fall forward or backward* (puts undue strain on muscles and joints), but always straight wide apart to sides. Keep back, shoulders, neck and head pinned to floor, not lifting as you spread legs wide.

Repeat the open-close action slowly *ten times*.

B-5 WALKING ON AIR

You get triple prime benefits: (a) strengthens abdominal and pelvic muscles; (b) tones extensor leg muscles; and (c) the flexes and extensions promote maximum mobility in hip and ankle joints. Start in B-1 position . . .

1. Lie flat on back, arms at sides, palms up . . . extend legs straight up at right angles to body, a few inches apart . . . ankles flexed as if feet were flat against ceiling. Breathe in and out regularly . . .

2. Point *left* foot upward (keeping right ankle flexed) . . . then

flex right ankle as at start, and *at same time* point left foot up. Flex each ankle and point foot in alternating rhythm *ten times* . . .

3. Keeping ankle-flexing pattern going, lower straight *right* leg forward about 12 to 14 inches, while keeping left leg up . . . then return right leg to starting position, and *at same time* lower straight *left* leg to similar angle.

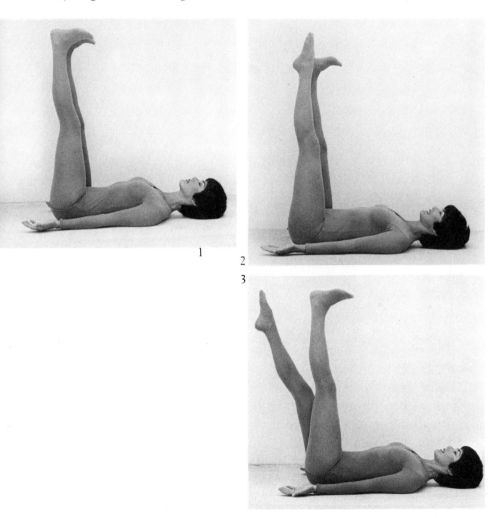

Continue alternating ankle-flexing actions as you alternate right and left leg movements *ten times each*, for a total of *twenty times*. Keep straight legs a few inches apart in ankle-hip alignment.

Enjoy the rhythmic alternating actions as you get into the swing.

B-6 UP-AND-AWAY

This fine conditioner improves leg and ankle circulation, flexibility and mobility, and strengthens leg, ankle joint, and foot muscles. Start in B-1 position . . .

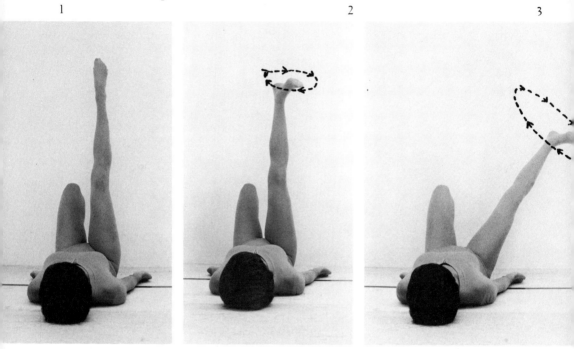

1. Lie on back, inhale . . . then exhale as you bring right leg straight up, knee locked, pointing toes toward ceiling . . . and *at the same time* flex your left knee and bring your left foot down flat on the floor, close in front of your left hip . . .

2. Breathing in and out deeply and naturally, keeping right leg straight, knee locked throughout, slowly rotate your right foot clockwise . . . complete the circle *five times* . . .

3. Continuing to rotate your right foot slowly, rotate your straight right leg clockwise *from the hip socket* in a twelve-inch circle. Repeat circle *five times*.

Reverse the position of your legs, so that your *left* leg is straight up, and your right foot is flat on the floor. Repeat the entire naturalaction, rotating your left ankle counterclockwise *five times*, then rotate your left leg counterclockwise *five times*, keeping the ankle circling too.

B-Special   TUCK ROLL TRANSITION

For your safety and best all-over conditioning, the Boutelle Method moves you from one natural-action to the next in a smooth flow, with no abrupt stress or strain on any parts of your body. You'll use the Tuck Roll Transition to go from B-6 to B-7, and in all lying-down natural-actions where you move from one side to the other (as in B-8 and B-9). It will become a natural movement for you, enhancing your flexibility and gracefulness in all your daily actions.

1. Lie on your back on the floor and *inhale* deeply as you pull your knees up over your chest, hands clasping just below knees, which are a few inches apart, aligned with your hip joints. Lift your head to tuck your chin on your chest, and look through your separated knees . . .

2a. *Exhale* as you lift your left hip and roll to your right side . . . pause, then extend right arm in straight alignment on floor, palm down . . . 2b. *extend* legs, aligned straight out on floor. At the same time, place left hand flat on floor about 10 to 12 inches in front of your chest, fingers parallel to your body . . .

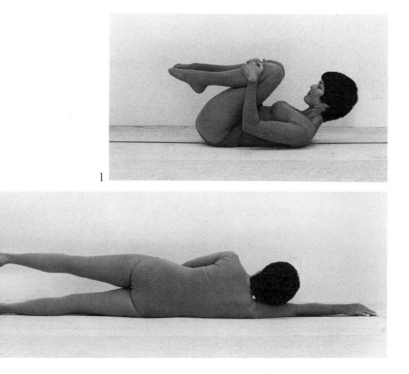

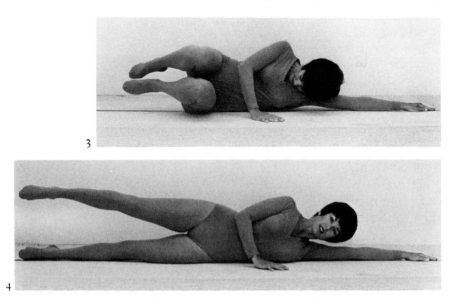

3

4

3. *Inhale* as you pull knees to your chest, a few inches apart . . . tuck your chin in against your chest, eyes focused between your knees. *Exhale* (blow!) as you lift *right* hip and roll over to your *left* side, using arms naturally to help your body roll smoothly.

4. Straighten out your legs and lift your head in straight alignment.

Repeat this smooth rolling action several times as practice, and enjoy the graceful movement as you master it. From now on it will take you safely and easily from one lying-down natural-action to another.

B-7   HANGING ON THE FLOOR

This side-lying arm stretch improves body alignment and balance, releases tension, and tones arm and leg muscles. You may find it somewhat difficult at first, but soon you will master the positioning and enjoy the super aligning and conditioning effect.

1. Pick a straight line on the floor—a floorboard, a straight carpet, tile or linoleum design, a rug seam, or an imaginary straight line (some students place a wide tape on a playroom floor). Lie on your *left* side, stretching out your body along the straight line. Stretch your legs so that your left ankle, knee and hip joints are centered on the floor line . . . along with your left arm socket, elbow, wrist joint and hand, palm against floor line; take your time getting into proper position.

Your straight *right* leg should be lifted a few inches to be parallel to the floor, aligned with right hip joint. Hold right arm out straight, a little over your right leg, parallel to the floor and aligned with your right shoulder . . . right palm facing upward. You are, in effect, "hanging" on the floor. *Inhale* deeply . . .

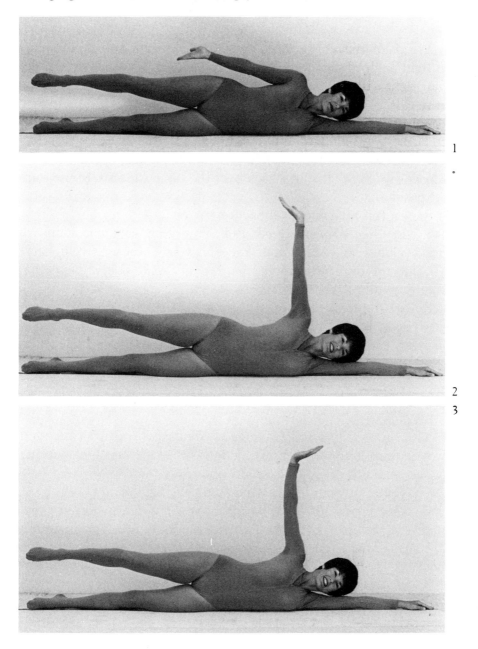

1

2

3

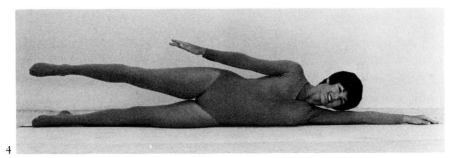

2. *Exhale* and slowly "blow" your straight right arm in an arc up to right angle alignment with your right side. As you move up, flex your right wrist and separate your fingers as though pushing air upward . . .

3. *Inhale* as you rotate your straight right arm by bringing palm up facing the ceiling, wrist flexed, fingers closed . . .

4. Reverse your straight right arm and hand action and exhale as you slowly "blow" the arm back over the same wide arc to the starting position.

Repeat this total double arc action *five times*.

5. Use the B-Special Tuck Roll Transition which is found on pages 89 and 90, pulling your knees to your chest with your hands . . . and roll over to position 1 but on your *right* side, straightening your body along the fixed line.

Repeat the total "hanging on the floor" action on your right side *five times*, as you did on your left side. (As a point of personal interest, you will find which is your "better" or stronger side in lateral ability, comparable with being right- or left-handed.)

B-8   SIDE-LYING LEG TWIST

This slow-twisting action increases the flexibility in your hip joints wonderfully, improves leg circulation, tones leg and foot muscles. Move naturally; don't strain at any point.

1. "Hang" on your *left* side, perfectly aligned as in B-7 . . .

2. Place your *right* hand flat on floor, palm down, ten to twelve inches in front of your chest, so that your right elbow is bent at a natural angle, and right hand on floor helps support your body.

3. *Inhale* and draw your right knee toward your right elbow . . .

4. *Exhale* as you draw your right knee up over your right hip, pointing right toe down to touch left leg . . .

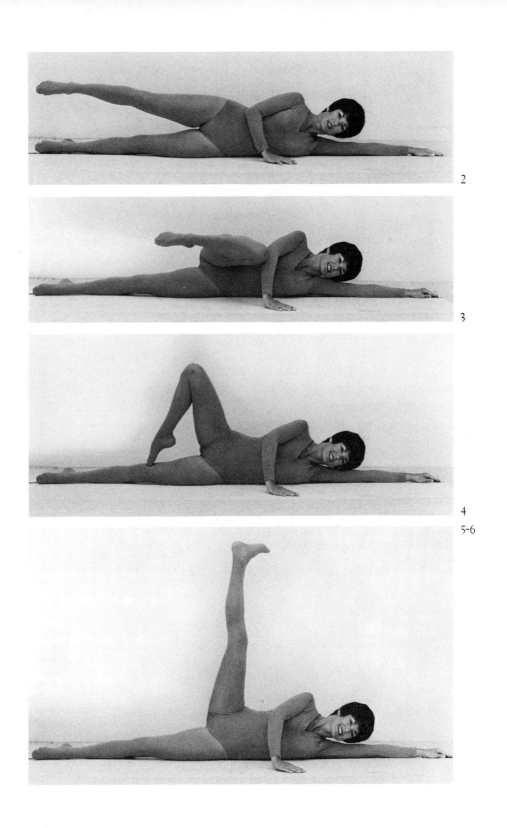

2

3

4

5-6

5. *Inhale* as you push your right leg as straight up as possible over your right hip . . . foot and toes pointed upward (you'll be able to straighten your leg up better week after week) . . . then

6. Flex your right ankle so the sole of your foot faces the ceiling, and stretch your toes wide apart as possible . . .

7. *Exhale* and slowly return your right leg back over hip, around to elbow repeating 4 and 3, and back to starting position in slow continuous action . . .

Repeat this entire action *five times*. Then use the B-Special Tuck Roll Transition to roll over to position 1 but on your *right* side. Repeat entire action on this side *five times*. (Pause to rest as and if needed—no strain or puffing.)

B-9   SIDE-LYING SWINGER

This natural-action increases the efficiency of the circulatory and respiratory systems, improves coordination, and tightens body balance and alignment.

1. Start as in B-8, but on your right side, aligned on a straight line . . .

2. *Inhale* deeply as you flex your left ankle and left knee, and draw your left heel toward your left hip joint and sitting muscles (gluteals). At the same time, flex your left elbow and bring your left hand forward, pacing it flat on the floor in front of your chest . . .

3. *Exhale* as you straighten your left leg and swing it forward in a straight path until toes touch the floor in front of your body (knee locked) . . .

4. *Inhale* as you swing your left leg back to starting position 1.

Repeat *five times*—be sure to think IN, think UP, and maintain your alignment throughout the swinging actions.

Then use the Tuck Roll Transition (pages 89–90) to roll over to position 1 but on your *left* side. Repeat entire action on left side *five times*. Don't overstrain at any point; see how remarkably your breathing, coordination, and graceful swinging actions improve week after week.

Note: Use the A-6 to A-7 Lying-to-Sitting Transition (page 71) when going from B-9 to B-10.

B-10 TIC-TAC-TOE

This will improve coordination of your knee and ankle joints and strengthen and firm back and shoulder muscle girdles.

1. Sit on floor, back straight, shoulder joints in alignment with hip sockets . . . straight arms (elbows locked) extended to sides in alignment with hip sockets, fingers touching floor . . . knees flexed with lower legs back as close as possible to thighs . . . feet flat on

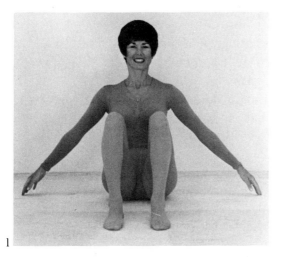

1

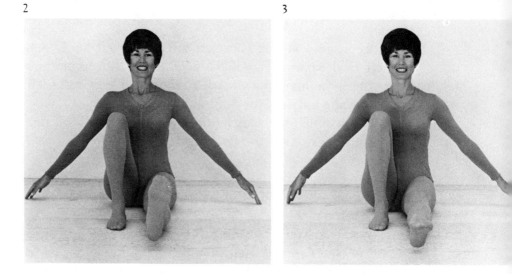

floor a few inches apart, aligned with hip sockets. *Breathe in* . . .

2. *Tic: Blow out* as you stretch *left* leg forward, flexing ankle so that toes point toward ceiling . . .

3. *Tac:* With left leg stretched forward, point left toes forward . . .

4. *Toe: Breathe in* as you flex left knee again and bring left leg back, foot on floor close to hip socket, as in starting position.

Now perform the same tic-tac-toe natural-action with right leg.

Alternate left and right leg flexing actions, *five each leg, ten times total*. Performing the actions with rhythmic motion, it's fun to say to yourself, "tic . . . tac . . . toe," in beat with each designated movement.

B-11   EMERGENCY BRAKE

These natural-actions strengthen and firm back and shoulder muscle girdles for proper alignment and endurance, as they activate joints and muscles of legs and arms.

1. Sit on floor with back straight, knees flexed a few inches apart, aligned with hip joints, feet flat on floor . . . hands clasping knees, elbows flexed, arms pulling lower legs as close to thighs as possible without straining. *Inhale* . . .

2. *Exhale* as you stretch right leg forward, knee locked, foot an inch above floor, ankle flexed so toes point up and foot presses forward as if pushing an emergency brake just above the floor . . .

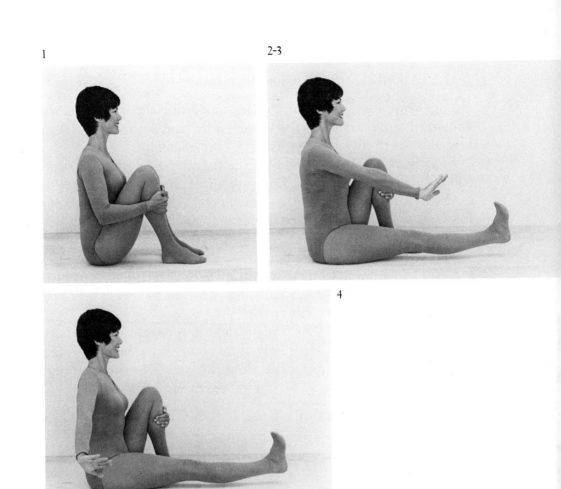

3. At the same time as you move *right leg* forward, move your right *arm* and hand pointed straight forward, elbow and wrist locked, parallel to floor . . .

4. Breathing regularly, turn palm of hand outward as though pushing away air . . . swing straight right arm in a continuous motion out to side and down until wrist joint is at height of hip socket a few inches above floor . . . then flex right elbow, and at the same time flex right knee, returning right leg to starting position, and returning hand to clasp leg again.

Do the same 2-3-4 actions with your *left* leg and arm. Alternate right and left legs and arms *five times each*, total of *ten times*.

These rhythmic natural-actions also improve your coordination for balanced body movement and control day in and day out.

B-12   TAILOR SIT PENDULUM SWING

This swing tones the vital muscles supporting the spinal column and arm muscles, tightens the pelvic girdle, and increases the flexibility of your trunk for greater balance and gracefulness.

1. Sit with legs crossed and tucked in front of your body . . . arms (elbows locked), hands and fingers pointed in straight alignment, extended to sides until fingertips touch floor naturally alongside your hip sockets. Inhale and exhale deeply and regularly throughout continuous pendulum actions . . .

2. Flex your *right* wrist and rotate your straight right arm so palm faces up . . . swing your right arm straight up at side to directly over your right shoulder joint as right palm (wrist flexed) exerts a lifting-pushing action . . .

3. Continue moving your straight right arm toward your *left* side so wrist is over left shoulder joint . . . as you flex and bend your *left* elbow toward your left hip socket, lowering your left forearm down to the floor, trunk bending in a natural arc to the left . . .

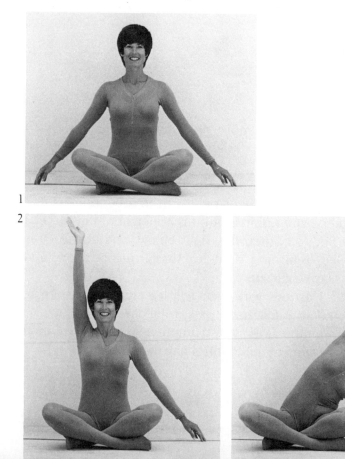

4   4A

4a. In a continuous pendulum swing, bring your straight *right* arm back straight up above your right shoulder joint . . . at same time lifting *left* forearm and straightening left elbow, flexing left wrist and rotating arm so palm faces up . . . 4b. lifting and pushing with left hand as left arm goes straight up at side to above left shoulder joint . . . and straight *right* arm returns to original position, fingertips touching floor . . . then flex right elbow and lower right forearm to floor, trunk bending naturally in an arc to the right . . . as you move your straight *left* arm up over your right shoulder joint.

5. Swing into original actions 2 and 3 again . . . then into action 4, resulting in another complete pendulum swing. Repeat the complete pendulum swings *ten times* in continuous smooth, graceful, slow rhythm. Be careful throughout not to lift off your sitting muscles . . . performing the actions smoothly and easily, not forcing. Stop any time you feel that you are straining.

You'll be thrilled as your actions smooth out and your energy increases, day after day, from repeating this super conditioner.

AFTER YOU HAVE MASTERED THE "B" PROGRAM

Your daily "B" session will develop and sustain your neuromuscular lifetime fitness to your maximum personal capacity. Since you are not competing with anyone, not trying to win any prizes (other than personal rewards from maximum fitness), nor attempting to become a Superwoman, you will attain the personal rewards of looking, feeling, and functioning at your best. There is no need or benefit to exerting beyond these superbly conditioning natural-actions.

You may wish to enjoy a ten-minute Boutelle session twice a day at times most convenient for you, as many enthusiasts do. Like others, you may wish to vary your sessions by mixing your personal favorite "A" and "B" natural-actions. You might also want to add or substitute some of the special *sports* actions (Chapter XI) and *problem spot* actions (Chapter XII).

Remember that you must continue your Boutelle sessions regularly in order to *stay* in top condition, for muscles weaken without sufficient usage. Enjoy sports, swimming, walking and other "fun" pursuits as you wish, but realize that there are no substitutes for all-over conditioning, which improves your skills, timing and endurance in whatever you do.

You will find yourself dealing better with everyday stress, helping to prevent and overcome common fatigue, reacting better in emergencies, and avoiding accidents and injuries due to lack of all-over muscular development, coordination and balance. Like so many thousands of my students, you are probably exclaiming at this point, "I look, feel, and function so much better that I wouldn't skip my Boutelle conditioning session for anything!"

IMPORTANT: Even if you haven't any special problem due to illness or injuries, I urge you to read the next chapter on the "M" Medical Referral Program, and *all* chapters, for two primary reasons:

1. If people you know are afflicted with lower back pains, arthritis, recent surgery, or other problems, you can point out that they may be able to get help, as so many others have who had despaired of becoming active again. My driving aim always is to help all people, in every condition, to look, feel, and function at their personal best. (They must always check with their physicians first, of course.)

2. If you should ever suffer an injury in an accident or otherwise, you will be aware of natural-actions that may be helpful to ease pain and stiffness, and promote speedy recovery. However, you must get your doctor's approval first, as I cannot assess your problem, which may include injuries such as broken bones.

IX
"M" Medical Referral Program for Special Problems

Through my years as a movement specialist, a number of physicians have referred patients to me for safe, effective physical therapy. They wanted patients to improve through my enjoyable natural-action methods, avoiding strenuous "exercise" and "calisthenics," which might do harm rather than good. I have helped individuals with many special problems such as pain and stiffness of the lower back, neck and shoulders; arthritis difficulties; mastectomy recovery; preparation for and speedier recovery after pregnancy and general surgery; strokes; joint problems, and more conditions that doctors knew could be alleviated through Boutelle natural-actions.

I cannot provide in this book all the natural-actions needed for all conditions. Many afflicted people must be treated individually. To help the greatest number, programs follow for the most common complaints—*lower back problems* and *arthritis*. I have added natural-actions for use following *mastectomy* since results have been so gratifying and the need for help is increasing.

Most people in my medical referral classes gain remarkable relief and mobility through "M" natural-actions, and ultimately progress to "A" and then "B" programs as they lose the fear of movement, and regain muscle elasticity and greater mobility. However, it is *essential* that you show your doctor this book and the natural-actions specified so that he or she will see exactly what you will be doing . . . *don't proceed without your physician's approval.*

LOWER BACK PAIN PROBLEMS

It is estimated that over 70,000,000 Americans—about one out of every three—have suffered from low-back pain and back-related ailments at some time. Many medical specialists affirm that most back problems relate to lack of proper physical conditioning, stating:

"Eighty-one percent of back pain is due to muscle weakness or inelasticity."

"The major reason for backache is weak abdominal muscles."

"By far the most common cause of chronic backache is postural."

"Specific exercises to strengthen the lower back muscles must be done every day."

"The most important single point to remember in backache is that sit-ups are not an abdominal exercise. They are a way of producing back pain."

Close to 80 percent of my medical referral students come for safe, effective backache relief and buildup against reoccurrence. I have found that the prime causes of backaches are flabby abdominal muscles and "layer-cake backs" with lower back muscles so lacking in elasticity (*tonus*) that they look like a three-layer cake. To restore muscles properly, it's necessary to conquer the tension and fear of moving, then to perform "M" natural-actions day after day to strengthen and regain elasticity in abdominal and pelvic girdle muscles, *as many Boutelle students have done.*

When pain is due to congenital defects (existing from birth but not hereditary), degenerative joint diseases such as osteoarthritis, herniated discs and the like, my aim always is to help you attain maximum mobility within your individual movement capacity as judged by your physician. You must adopt the cautious "how much is right for me" attitude. You may have a "teacup back" that, like a mended teacup, is highly vulnerable to another knock, and you must treat your teacup back respectfully in all activities. Take it slowly and easily with rhythmic natural-actions for wonderful relief and improvement. Never overexert; your guideline is *do . . . but don't overdo.*

"M" SAFETY LIE-DOWN TRANSITION

For the person with lower back trouble, carelessly going from standing to lying down may cause problems. This Boutelle safe way makes it easy and graceful to get down on your back for the "M" program:

1. Stand a few feet in front of a blank wall space, next to a heavy piece of furniture such as an armchair, table, or couch. Always perform all actions slowly for steadiness and control.

2. With one hand on furniture for support, bend your knees and place one knee and then the other on the floor so you are kneeling.

3. Place one hand, then the other, on the floor so that each wrist is under its respective shoulder, arms straight, in the basic all-fours position A-10 (Chapter VII).

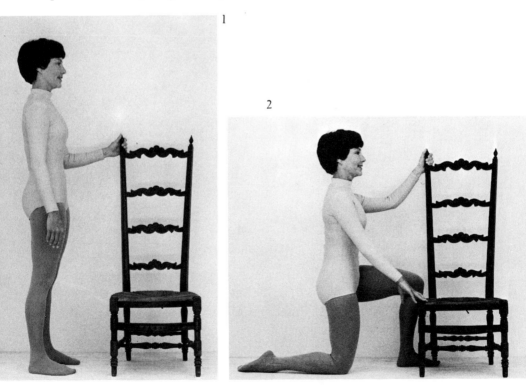

1

2

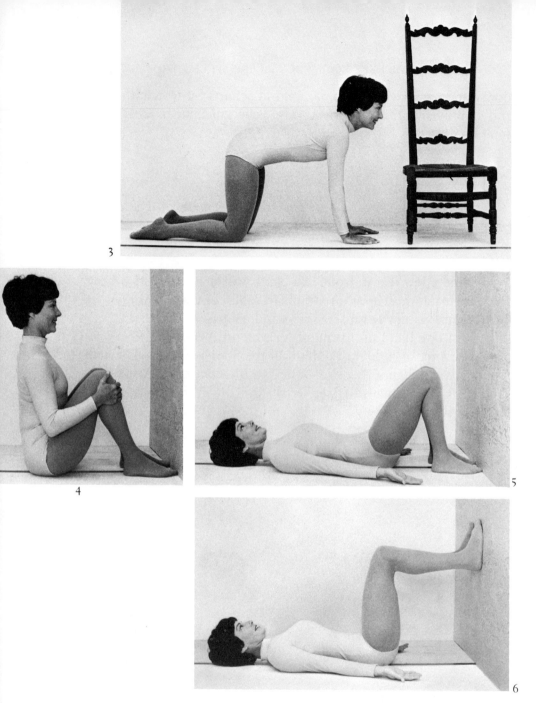

4. Slowly roll over on your right hip and sit on floor in tuck-sit position A-7 (Chapter VII), hands holding your knees. Check that your feet are a few inches apart so that ankle, knee, hip and shoulder joints are in correct alignment, giving you solid support.

5. Now place each hand under and behind its respective knee

joint . . . keep feet firmly on the floor as your hands slide slowly down the backs of your legs toward your hips and lend support as you carefully roll down your spinal column until your back is settled on the floor, then place arms at your sides. You are now in the basic A position (Chapter VII), with the blank wall in front of your feet.

6. Bring your right foot and then your left foot up against the wall so that you are now in basic M-1 position, firmly and confidently supported by your back flat on the floor and feet against the wall— ready to go into the series of "M" natural-actions.

Important: As you begin the "M" program, perform each natural-action *three to five times each*, depending on your personal capacity and comfort. Gradually, over a period of weeks, increase to a maximum of *ten repetitions* of each natural-action.

M-1   TENSION RELEASE

Your first natural-action could hardly be simpler or easier. All you need is a floor and a little clear wall space . . .

1. Lie on your back comfortably in basic M position . . . knees flexed so upper legs are at right angles to floor, lower legs parallel to floor . . . feet flat against wall, a few inches apart for proper alignment of ankle joints with knee joints and hip sockets. Keep your back snugly against floor throughout. Place left arm relaxed close to your left side, palm up . . . place right hand flat on your lower abdominal muscles . . .

2. Now inhale and exhale very slowly and deeply: breathe in through your nose . . . blow out through your mouth.

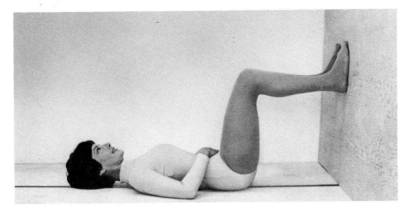

That's all there is to it—close your eyes as you inhale-exhale very slowly, each time more deeply and slowly. Feel a sense of supported back, relaxed shoulder and neck muscles . . . and note how the abdominal muscles pull away from your hand as you inhale, then rise as you exhale. That simple deep-breathing action in this position, practically effortless, is helping to activate and strengthen your abdominal muscles as it releases body tension all over.

M-2 KNEE-LEG ACTIVATOR

In same position as M-1, you begin to activate and tone your leg muscles, and improve flexibility of your hip, knee, and ankle joints, along with strengthening abdominal and pelvic girdle muscles. Again, easy does it . . .

1. Lie in basic position, this time with both arms relaxed close to your sides, palms up . . .

2. *Inhale* deeply as you slowly draw your right knee, toes pointed

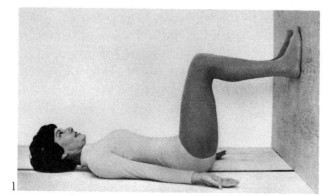

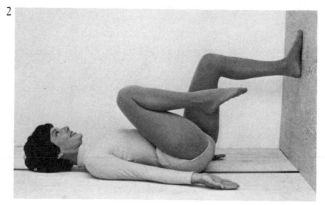

forward, back toward your right shoulder . . . keeping lower leg parallel to the floor . . . slowly pulling leg back as far as possible without straining at all . . .

3. *Exhale* (blow!) as you flex your right ankle so that sole of your foot is parallel to the wall . . . and slowly return leg to starting position.

Do the same with your left leg. Alternate right and left leg actions slowly and carefully, inhaling and exhaling deeply.

M-3   TWO LEGS ACTIVATOR

1. In same position as M-2, you will be further toning abdominal and leg muscles and joints . . .

2. *Inhale* deeply as you slowly draw both knees *at the same time* back toward the respective shoulders . . . toes pointed forward, lower legs parallel to the floor. Double-check to be sure ankles and knees are a few inches apart so that joints are in supportive natural alignment. Draw back both knees as far as you can but without stress or strain (each week your legs will attain greater flexibility without tension) . . .

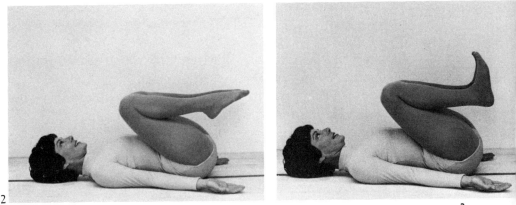

2   3

3. *Exhale* as you flex both ankles so that soles of feet are parallel to the wall . . . and slowly return legs to starting position, feet against wall.

As you repeat the total actions, feel the strengthening, firming effect in your abdominal and pelvic girdle muscles.

M-4   DOUBLE SPINE STRENGTHENER

Your cervical (neck) and lumbar (between lower ribs and pelvis) areas are flexible and vulnerable, and they interact. Therefore it is necessary to strengthen both, as in this valuable natural-action.

1. Lie in same basic position as M-2, keeping your arms and shoulders snugly in holding position against the floor throughout. *Inhale* deeply as you *very slowly* lift your head to focus your gaze through the "window" between your knees (which, of course, are a few inches apart in correct alignment . . .

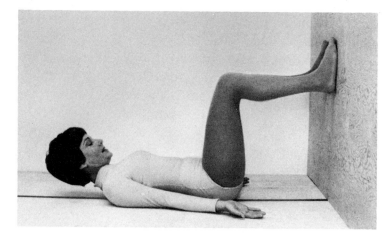

2. *Blow air out* as you very slowly return your head to starting position on floor.

As you perform repeats of the total action, be sure to move your head slowly and comfortably, without tension or strain.

M-5   WALK-UP-THE-WALL

Here you strengthen essential abdominal and leg muscles with differing actions from a different approach.

1. Lie in M-4 starting position and *inhale*.
2. *Exhale* as you "walk" both legs up the wall—right, left, right, left—until legs (in alignment a few inches apart) are fully extended . . . toes pointed upward as close to the wall as comfortable for you, heels resting against the wall . . .
3. *Inhale* as you flex your right ankle so the sole of your foot faces

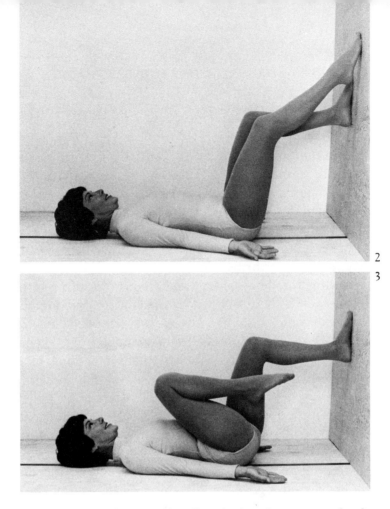

2

3

toward the ceiling . . . flex knee and pull right leg down very slowly so that your knee socket is over your chest . . . then *exhale* as you point right toes forward and return your right leg slowly to starting point, flexing right ankle so your foot is flat against the wall.

Perform same action with your left leg, then repeat all actions.

After at least four weeks of daily "M" actions, if you feel thoroughly comfortable with your daily session, no strain at all, proceed with the "A" program (Chapter VII) this way: For the two following weeks, add A-1, A-2, A-3. Two weeks later add A-4, A-5, A-6. Two weeks later add A-7, A-8, A-9. Two weeks later add A-10, A-11, A-12. *Always start each daily session with the entire "M" series.* By the time you are doing the entire program with no stress at all, you can drop the "M" series, and eventually move on to the "B" program, as your capacity dictates. Always go very carefully, stopping at the slightest sign of discomfort or strain.

ARTHRITIS—RELIEF AND FUNCTIONAL HELP

Important to ALL readers: The Arthritis Foundation states that "Arthritis is often called 'everybody's disease.' It affects every one of us in some way. . . . Yet most people have only hazy ideas—and often incorrect ideas—of what it's all about. . . . They don't understand that arthritis is never hopeless."

By promoting proper posture and movement, even though you may not have arthritis, Boutelle natural-actions are helpful toward preventing the development and effects of arthritis, especially pertinent to you if there is a history of arthritis affliction in your family.

The chronic, disabling disease of arthritis ("inflammation of a joint") is more prevalent among women than men. Combining *gentle*, especially created and basic natural-actions, I have been able to help many afflicted individuals of varying ages in our Medical Referral classes. They have gained considerable relief from pain, along with improved movement and functioning, as many had never thought possible. One of my successful students calls my method "the healing art of gentle persuasion."

A typical instance is Barbara M., a beautiful woman of 42. Leaning heavily on a cane, hardly able to walk, she hobbled in one day and explained that she had been suffering from rheumatoid arthritis for several years. She had heard glowing reports from others about relief through the Boutelle Method, and she asked desperately, "Can you help me?"

"I'll try," I said, "with your doctor's permission, and with your total cooperation in helping yourself by following instructions faithfully." I explained why: "I designed Boutelle natural-actions to improve and maintain the *functioning power* of every joint in the body, so vital with arthritis. We also stress *proper positioning* of joints through *postural alignment*. And we promote both through safe, gentle natural-actions. Here are the key guidewords: *gentle . . . patient . . . persistent.*"

Her physician approved (he had referred other patients who had benefited), and Barbara started her program with determination and hope. At this writing, six months later, she walks well without a cane. She does her own housework. She calls the wonderful change a "miracle," but I credit her courage and intelligent persistence, along with gentle, corrective natural-actions. If you will work faithfully day after day with the program as instructed here (always with your doctor's approval), chances are excellent that it will work for you—just as it has helped many others suffering from mild to acute rheumatoid arthritis and osteoarthritis, as well as some other forms of this disabling disease.

Boutelle Anti-Arthritis Program

Caution: Don't attempt to do all the natural-actions if at any time your joints are highly inflamed and painful. Wait for remission, then start again.

Your program begins by sitting in a straight, hard chair without arms. First you must learn proper sitting alignment, as instructed in Chapter III. Don't minimize the importance of correct Boutelle posture sitting and standing. Practice proper sitting and standing alignment right now, and remain aware from now on—always think IN, think UP.

Before proceeding, please be sure that you have read the first four chapters thoroughly. It would be best if you reread them now for deep understanding of the all-over benefits and necessity for all-over body conditioning for you as well as for everyone else, afflicted or not.

If your condition prevents you from sitting in correct alignment right away, keep trying until you are able to and it becomes natural for you. Remember that proper positioning of the joints in sitting, standing, and moving is one of the most significant points in helping to overcome arthritis pain, stiffness, and limited function.

Take some extra moments now to practice *rhythmic-flow breathing*, as instructed in Chapter IV. Realize that every time you "blow like a whale," you expel carbon dioxide most effectively. You will be progressing from the inside out toward your goal of all-over neuromuscular fitness now and for your lifetime. Rhythm-flow breathing in correct posture alignment also helps to relieve *tension*, which is a prime enemy of the arthritis victim. All natural-actions are created to combat tension and stiffness, as they induce smooth, strain-free *movement* to try to loosen and banish the grip of arthritis as much as possible.

Please try to enjoy Boutelle natural-actions, as others do. Make it fun! As you proceed with each daily session, tell yourself: "I know I can . . . I know I can . . . " Don't be discouraged at the start or as you go along. Regardless of how tight or stiff or awkward you feel, I have probably helped worse conditions than yours in our classes. Keep trying and, like Barbara M., chances are that you too can perform a personal "miracle" transformation. No matter what, you will be trying, and in my experience trying is more than half of winning.

How many times? Perform every natural-action *three to five times or less* at the start, depending on your personal capacity—you must be the judge. Never forget your key guideword: *gentle*. Never force yourself; be patient about progressing little by little. Gradually, over a period of at least six weeks or more, you may increase to a maximum of *ten repetitions* of each natural-action as you feel that you can without straining.

M-6 UPPER JOINTS MOBILIZERS A-B-C

These natural-actions all improve mobility in your fingers, wrists, elbows, shoulders—as they tone the muscles which lend support to the joints. Do all movements very slowly and gently, no straining or forcing at any time. Repeat each Mobilizer *three to five times*, but stop at any point if it's a strain—time enough to increase the number of repetitions on following days, as you will be able to gradually.

MOBILIZER A: 1. Sit as perfectly aligned as possible for you in a straight chair (check correct sitting alignment in Chapter II). Flex your elbows, keeping elbows tucked to your sides, flexed at right angles to your body . . . palms facing up and away at your sides, fingers spread (you should not be able to see your arms) . . . now *exhale (blow!)* . . .

2. *Inhale deeply* as you pull your lower arms up and wrap your spread fingers around respective shoulder cap muscles (or as close to that as you can) while keeping elbows close to your sides. Now *exhale* as you lower your arms to the starting position.

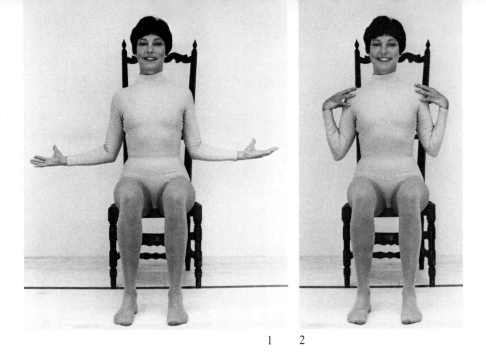

1   2

MOBILIZER B: 1. Sit in same starting position as Mobilizer A
. . . *exhale* as you flex your wrists and push your arms away from
your sides until elbows lock and wrists are aligned with your hip
sockets . . . then curl your fingers into fists (as well as you can) . . .

    2. *Inhale* slowly as you open your fingers and return your arms to
the starting position.

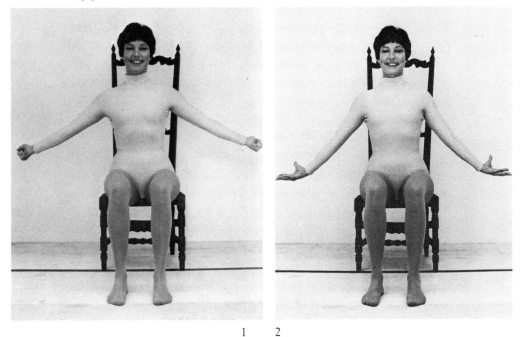

1   2

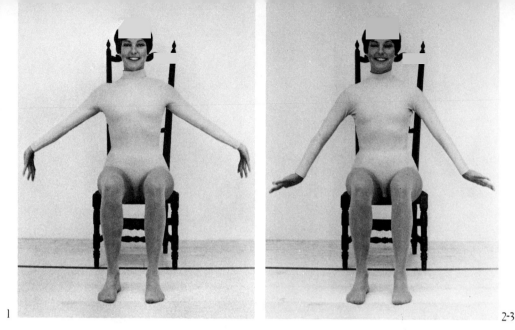

MOBILIZER C: 1. In same starting position, *exhale* as you flex your wrists and push arms out to your sides with the heel of each hand until elbows lock and wrists are aligned with your hip sockets . . .

2. *Inhale* slowly as you gently rotate your straight arms in your shoulder sockets 180° in a back, up and away direction so your palms are facing up and away from your body (gently, not forcing) . . .

3. *Exhale* as you spread your fingers and scratch the air energetically, using all your finger joints vigorously as much as possible. Then *inhale* slowly as you rotate your arms forward so that palms face up . . . and pull arms back to the starting position.

Your arm muscles and joints will have benefited considerably (more so day by day) from this effective series of all-over toning and conditioning Mobilizers, a fine start.

M-7 LEG JOINTS MOBILIZER

You should not be wearing shoes for this vital natural-action, which helps your hip, knee, ankle and toe joints and supporting muscles. Perform all actions gently, slowly . . .

1. Sit perfectly aligned in chair . . . arms at your sides with elbows flexed comfortably as you clasp the seat of the chair on each side . . . *inhale* as you flex your *right* knee, right foot pointed downward, and bring right leg up slowly as high as you can without straining, so that upper thigh leaves chair seat (keep shoulders quiet, not rising, relaxed and in alignment over hips) . . .

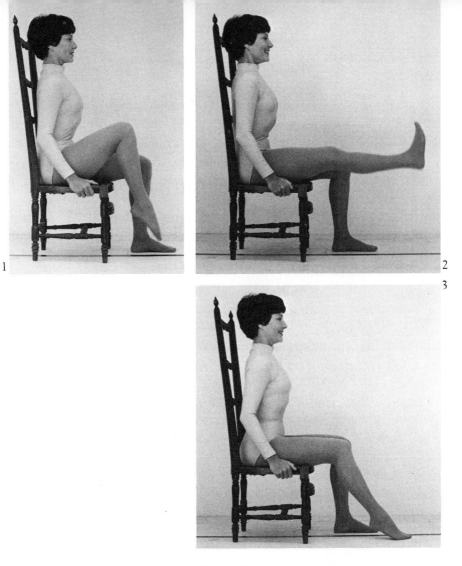

2. *Exhale*, and flex your right ankle so toes point upward as you slowly stretch your right leg forward in as straight a line as possible with your hip socket, until your knee locks gently . . . and spread your toes out as wide as you can (ankle still flexed) . . .

3. *Inhale*, and keeping right leg straight . . . lower leg as you reach for the floor with the ball of your right foot . . .

4. *Exhale*, as you flex right knee and bring right foot back to starting position in alignment on the floor.

Repeat same action with your *left* leg. Alternate right and left leg actions, proceeding gently, taking your time, never overstraining.

Keep in mind the basic Boutelle rule that if you feel fatigued at any point, STOP. Resume if you wish when you feel rested.

Remain seated in your chair in correct alignment . . . think IN, think UP. Now turn back to Chapter VII, the "A" Alpha Program. You will do some of the "A" natural-actions, but seated in your chair, *not on the floor*. You can readily adapt the movements in your well-supported sitting position, less demanding at this stage of your conditioning. As with M-6 and M-7, perform the actions only a few times at the start, gradually working up to the full "A" instructions—but only after weeks of daily sessions, and only after you can do the full number of repetitions smoothly, easily, with no strain at all. Now proceed with:

A-7   GENTLE NECK STRETCH (pages 71–72) Do this seated on the chair with your arms at your sides comfortably.

A-8   ROWING ACTION (pages 73–74) Perform the rowing action with your arms while seated in chair . . . but keep your feet in their aligned position on the floor, not moving your feet at all.

A-9   THE WAVE (pages 74–75) You do this conditioner seated in alignment in your chair. The action gently flexes your spine and spinal muscles in smooth, rhythmic flow, firming your midriff too. Keep your feet firmly on the floor throughout.

Reminder: *Gentle* is your guideword in performing all natural-actions. As I keep repeating to Boutelle classes, "What benefits you most is *how* you perform movements, not how many times."

After at least four to eight weeks on your daily anti-arthritis program, if you are feeling in easy full control, performing all these natural-actions smoothly and comfortably in your chair, *check with your physician* for permission to move on to the full "A" program in the "A" positions on the floor (show your doctor the actions in the book).

You'll be happy to learn that the majority of my arthritis students advance and are able to perform the full "A" program eventually, as practice improves movement and ability remarkably. But don't ever force yourself—be gentle, patient, and savor the delight of improving little by little.

When you have the doctor's permission to move on to the "A" program, begin every daily session with M-6 and M-7, then expand to the full "A" program (Chapter VII) this way:

For the first two weeks, add A-1, A-2, A-3.

If you are performing easily, add A-4, A-5, A-6.

After two weeks, add A-7, A-8, A-9 in full "A" positions, not on chair.

Two weeks later, add A-10, A-11, A-12. When you are doing the entire "A" program smoothly and easily, you can drop M-6 and M-7 if you wish.

Like a number of my students who started in Medical Referral classes, then moved into "A" classes, eventually you may go on to the "B" program . . . but only if you are confident of your capacity, and with your doctor's approval. You will be overjoyed to have brought about your personal "miracle." *Congratulations!*

SPEEDING MASTECTOMY RECOVERY

Physicians send an increasing number of women to my Medical Referral classes after mastectomy surgery because of the gratifying results achieved by so many women. (Often patients have already started movement therapy before leaving the hospital.) My specially created mastectomy natural-actions are designed to help each participant regain maximum motion as quickly as possible, providing emotional as well as physical benefits. Many students go on to attain even greater all-over neuromuscular fitness than before, once they discover the Boutelle Method.

Especially in the early stages of the mastectomy program, my repeated caution always is to stop "at the edge of the hurt." Never forget that basic instruction. Before you start, get your physician's approval; point out in this book the natural-actions you will be doing. (I recommend that all mastectomy patients investigate early the fine Reach to Recovery Program of the American Cancer Society.)

Begin your program by practicing correct alignment sitting and standing (Chapter III), and rhythm-flow breathing (Chapter IV). Please reread the first four chapters for thorough understanding about reaching your dual goals of recovery and lifetime fitness.

How many times? Perform natural-actions *three to five times* or less at the start, depending on your personal capacity, never straining. Gradually over a period of four to six weeks or more, you may increase to as many as *ten repetitions* of your "M" natural-actions, and eventually up to the maximum stated for "A" and "B" actions.

Your Mastectomy Program

M-6   UPPER JOINTS MOBILIZER

Follow instructions (see pages 112–114 and 105–106) to improve mobility, tone muscles and joints of your upper body, and relieve tension.

M-8 THE SWINGER

This excellent natural-action strengthens arm muscles and the vital fan-shaped *pectoralis* muscles in the chest.

1. Sit in the correct alignment on a straight, hard chair . . . elbows flexed, hands on shoulder caps as in M-6 . . . *inhale* . . .

2. Flex your wrists and *exhale* as you slowly straighten your arms, lock your elbows, and push your arms out to the sides, wrists leading the way, fingers pointing down toward the floor, pushing hard with your hands as though moving heavy objects away from your body . . . until your wrists are level with your hip sockets.

3. Then *inhale* as you cup your hands, palms up, flex elbows, and return to starting position with hands on shoulder caps . . .

4. *Exhale* as your hands stay on shoulder caps and slowly swing your flexed elbows directly forward and up to shoulder height . . . and in continuing slow action *inhale* and swing your arms back to starting position with hands on shoulder caps and elbows at sides . . .

5. *Exhale* and with hands holding shoulder caps, swing your elbows out to the sides with insides of arms facing forward, so that at top of swing elbows are level with your arm sockets . . . then, in continuing slow action, *inhale* and return arms to starting position.

Repeat all steps *five times*.

Keep your feet fixed in alignment position on the floor throughout, and keep your knees, shoulders and hips in alignment position as you sit. Don't force anything; remember to move only to the

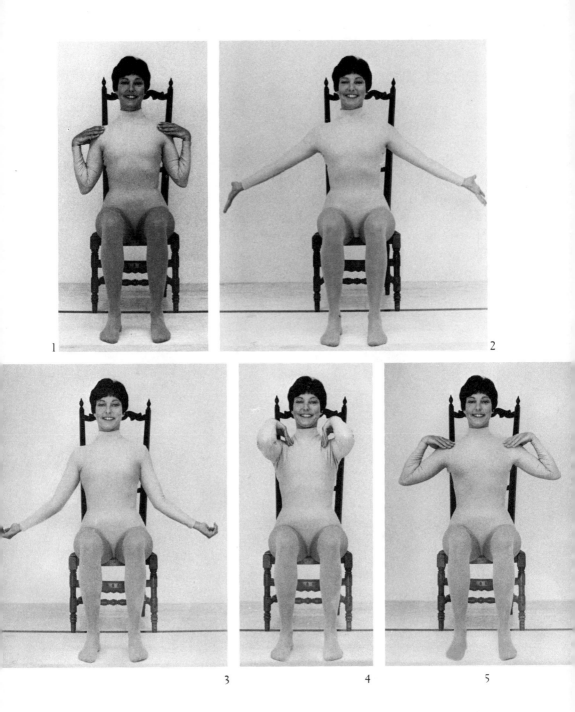

1

2

3

4

5

"edge of the hurt." At the start, your forward and side swings can be
minimal; you'll be thrilled as your mobility improves day after day,
and your range of action increases smoothly and comfortably. *Run
smooth* in all your actions—no straining.

M-9 PICTURE FRAME

This smooth, graceful natural-action is pretty as a picture as it tones and strengthens essential chest, shoulder, and arm muscles and joints.

1. Stand in Boutelle alignment with hands resting on your shoulder caps as in M-6 and M-8 . . . think IN, think UP. *Inhale* as you bring arms up slowly, flexing elbows, and rest your right palm on top of your head . . . and left palm "sealed" over back of right hand. Keep elbows straight out at sides so you can't see them out of the corners of your eyes . . . and keep shoulders at rest, not hunched up . . .

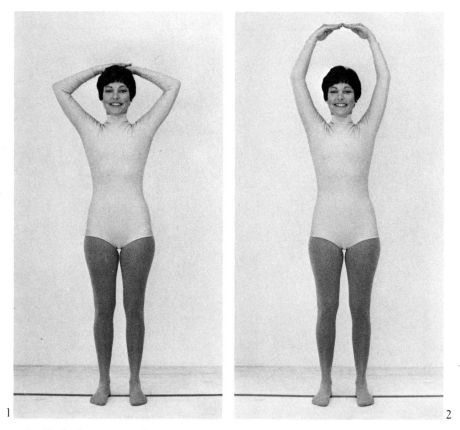

1   2

2. *Exhale* as you bring arms up slowly and touch fingertips of both hands (not interlocking) to form an oval "picture frame" for your head . . . keep elbows pointed out at sides, not bending for-

ward. In bringing arms up to make the oval frame, go up only as high as you can comfortably (you will improve wonderfully week by week).

3. *Inhale* as you return to position 1 with hands on top of head . . . *exhale* as you return to position 2, making oval frame.

Repeat head-frame actions *three to five times*, no forcing, then return arms to basic standing alignment.

Note: At first you may be able to attain starting position 1 only very slowly, but realize that this is a real beginning, and just proceed gently and gradually until you can reach the position easily.

M-10   FORWARD SWING

This superb body conditioner provides an exhilarating feeling of full-length toning, especially effective for chest, arms, shoulders, abdomen.

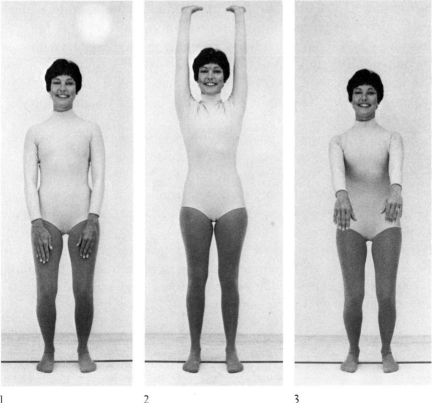

1   2   3

1. Stand in basic Boutelle alignment . . . place palms of hands on upper thighs . . . *exhale* as you bend knees slightly . . .

2. Swing arms very slowly straight forward and up, straightening legs in rhythm as your arms move up . . . backs of hands, facing forward, lead your arms up, but as your straight arms reach shoulder height on the way up, flex your wrists back and point your fingers back so that at the top your palms are parallel with the ceiling . . .

3. *Inhale* as you very slowly retrace your up-actions . . . straightening wrists and bending knees slightly again in rhythm as you lower arms to starting position. (Note that you are *blowing* arms up, and *inhaling* them down.)

Repeat total up-down actions *three to five times* . . . always without straining, never past "the edge of the hurt," and very slowly—remember that the good, as in all Boutelle natural-actions, is in *how* you move, not how *fast* you move.

After four to eight weeks on the mastectomy recovery program, performing the four natural-actions smoothly and comfortably, check with your physician for permission to move on to the full "A" program (show your doctor the program in this book). With approval, continue daily with M-6, M-8, M-9, M-10 . . . and add a few "A" actions every two weeks until you have added the entire "A" program—but never straining or pushing beyond your comfortable capacity.

The great majority of my mastectomy recovery students become very enthusiastic about how speedily and comfortably they return to normal. They are so happy about how the total body conditioning helps them look and feel much better emotionally as well as physically, that they go on from "A" to the "B" program, and continue on for lifetime fitness.

I must admit that some of the greatest gratification I get from my fitness work is seeing women after mastectomy surgery becoming not just as well as before but *much more fit* in many cases, and with a wonderful new optimistic outlook.

VITAL BODY CONDITIONING AFTER CHILDBIRTH . . . HYSTERECTOMY . . . VARIED SURGERY

This is essential information for you whether or not you expect to be hospitalized in the near future: Reports from many students in my classes, and from their physicians, furnish overwhelming proof that inside-out neuromuscular conditioning aids women greatly in undergoing childbirth, hysterectomy, and various other kinds of surgery . . . and helps them recover and return to normality more comfortably and speedily.

These are added sound reasons why you should be faithful to your daily program to help prevent troubles and to handle them better if they arise. As for recovery from such a surgical procedure, keep checking your physician for permission to start your reconditioning program. With approval (show this book), begin slowly and carefully . . .

First . . . practice Boutelle sitting alignment and standing alignment (Chapter III), and rhythmic-flow breathing (Chapter IV) . . . never forgetting in all your actions daily to think IN, think UP. Then perform the following natural-actions daily, starting with up to *three times* each, then after a few weeks increasing to the number of times specified in the instructions for each procedure. Remember that if you feel tired or strained at any point, STOP. Try again tomorrow. (All the following are in Chapter VII.)

A-1 THE CINCH: Strengthens muscles of your legs and midriff area . . . firms the abdomen, waist, hips, buttocks.

A-4 BOUTELLE NO-STRAIN PELVIC TILT: Designed specifically to strengthen the internal muscles of the lower digestive track, and your pelvic area and leg muscles—*without strain*.

A-10 KITTEN CURL: This graceful, enjoyable, favorite natural-action functions to help you recuperate three primary ways: (a) strengthens pelvic girdle muscles while relaxing tension in shoulder girdle muscles; (b) establishes correct spinal alignment and strengthens muscles supporting the spine; and (c) eases tension in the cervical spine, and aids toning and circulation all over body.

After four weeks or more of performing these natural-actions daily, or twice daily if you feel strong and eager, not overdoing . . . ask your doctor's approval to move on to the complete "A" program, perhaps in gradual steps, adding a few more natural-actions every two or three weeks . . . and eventually to the "B" program, when you have advanced that far and are ready to develop up to your personal maximum capacity for lifetime fitness.

HIGH BLOOD PRESSURE . . . STROKES . . . HEART DISEASE . . . VARIED AFFLICTIONS

The basic Boutelle program for lifetime fitness is designed not only to condition you for your maximum personal health, but also to help you combat the prime killers—high blood pressure (hypertension), strokes, heart disease—and other varied ills. Maintaining your top neuromuscular fitness always is a valuable preventive aid.

If you have high blood pressure, common in strokes, heart disease, and many other problems, you can help control it with natural-action conditioning and rhythmic breathing—always with your doctor's approval beforehand. (We have cooperated with health associations in taking blood pressure readings before and after classes, with gratifying results.) In addition to your daily program, here are added quick, simple, effective tips:

• *Any time you feel frustrated and uptight*, take a moment to do this: First, "blow like a whale" through your mouth, forcing out carbon dioxide waste, blowing right from the bottom of your lungs . . . then breathe in deeply, through your nose . . . blow out . . . breathe in . . . slowly, deeply, repeating out-in *five times*. You will start to feel relaxed emotionally and physically, and you will gain renewed energy. Always do this rhythmic breathing smoothly, without strain—empty your mind as well as your lungs as you blow out, concentrating on your breathing—then refill fully with air as you think IN, think UP always, for a sure quick pick-up.

• *If you have a pounding headache*, this action usually brings rapid relief: Standing or sitting in correct alignment (preferably sitting in the recommended position on the floor), close your eyes . . .

breathe deeply and rhythmically as you perform the A-7 Gentle Neck Stretch (Chapter VII). Do it immediately at the onset of the headache—don't wait for it to clamp down. Realize that headaches are varied and involve many complications, and while the Gentle Neck Stretch is not offered as a "cure," it usually brings some easing of pressure and pain with most headaches. Act fast, stop whatever you are doing, and perform the natural-action.

• *Whenever you feel "ready to scream,"* as problems and frustration build steam, stop and treat yourself to a brief recess as you perform the Two Quick Neuromuscular Anytime Energizers in Chapter V. It should help you to calm down and start "running smooth" in no time at all.

• *When you are about to "blow up,"* nerves jangled, feeling as though blood is about to spout through the top of your head, you need all-over relaxation and conditioning at once. Whatever you are doing, break away and find a private spot. After a couple of minutes of *rhythmic-flow breathing*, get down on the floor (go ahead, it's important to your health and total well-being), and do the A-4 Boutelle No-Strain Pelvic Tilt . . . then follow with A-10 Kitten Curl (both in Chapter VII). This brief session is practically "guaranteed" to ease tension, soothe your system, and make you feel better all over.

Proved Help in Many Afflictions

After an individual has had a stroke, a heart attack, or other serious medical problem, the course of treatment in every aspect must be directed by the personal physician, of course. In Boutelle classes, we have helped many people referred to us by their doctors—victims of mild strokes of various kinds, those with heart problems of different kinds, and other ills.

For example, it is not unusual for a woman using a pacemaker to participate in and benefit from the Boutelle Method (always with her doctor's permission). If you are a victim of hypertension, stroke, heart disease, or other ailments, please show this book to your physician, get his full recommendation, then move ahead with the "A" Alpha Program cautiously and safely, never straining or overdoing, to obtain the same benefits that others are enjoying daily.

NATURAL-ACTIONS FOR OTHER COMMON PROBLEMS

Note this list of some common problems, with natural-actions that are often helpful. Do them *extra-slowly* . . . and if you feel any strain or pain, STOP. (In the listing below, all the "Q" actions are in Chapter V; all the "A" actions are in Chapter VII; the "M" actions are earlier in this chapter.)

HEADACHES: Q-1, Q-2, A-7, A-10, M-9.

MODERATE NECK PAIN: Q-1, Q-2, A-7, A-9, A-10, M-9.

SORE SHOULDERS, UPPER ARMS: Remember to keep elbows IN (Chapter X), A-9, M-6, M-8, M-9, M-10.

"TENNIS/GOLF ELBOW," LOWER ARMS, WRISTS: Remember to keep elbows IN (Chapter X), A-8, M-6–A-B-C, M-8, S-5 (Chapter XI).

HAND STIFFNESS, PAIN; M-6–B-C.

LOWER BACK PAIN: M-1, M-2, M-3, M-4, M-5.

SORE LEGS, KNEE STIFFNESS, PAIN: M-2, M-3, M-5, M-7.

ANKLE STIFFNESS, PAIN: G-8 (Chapter XIII).

FOOT ACHES AND PAINS: F-1, F-2, F-3 (Chapter X).

ACTION NOW: THE KEY TO YOUR FUTURE

To help keep these ills and others from striking you, and for better control if you have a problem, *now is the time* to start and maintain your natural-action conditioning program daily . . . to breathe correctly . . . to eat properly for full health and to counteract overweight . . . to obtain adequate rest and relaxation . . . to have medical checkups regularly without fail. While all your difficulties cannot be prevented, you will have a far better chance for lasting good health.

Think of the alternatives: A wise man was asked for advice about a much-used path along the edge of a steep cliff—it was dangerous but provided a magnificent view. One alternative, he said, would be to build a strong fence; another would be to keep an ambulance at the foot of the cliff . . .

We urge you to take positive, health-building protective action for yourself now—and *keep it up daily* to enjoy your maximum lifetime fitness.

X

Daily Living Actions to Improve Posture, Energy, Endurance

There is a healthful, correct way, and many potentially harmful ways, to use your limbs and entire body in the usual everyday actions—walking and sitting, bending, driving and riding in a car, lifting objects, and so on. How you handle such common actions can result in "running smoothly" all day, or suddenly groaning, "Oh, my aching back!" after bending or reaching improperly. Here are your guidelines for correct natural-actions that will help you perform better and prevent trouble. All are a vital part of developing and maintaining lifetime fitness. Practice them right now, and make them part of your graceful, attractive movements from now on.

BOUTELLE BENDING-DOWN ACTION

From now on, *don't just bend down any which way*—straight-legged from your hips, with widespread splayed feet, or with other incorrect actions that often cause injury and pain. Whether you are picking up something from the floor, getting an object from a low shelf,

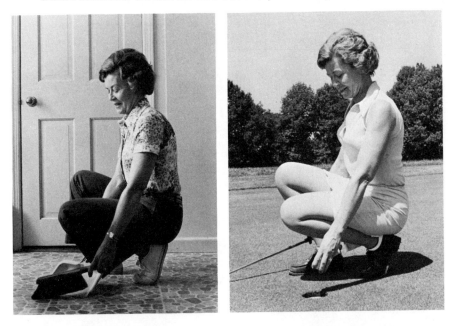

plugging in the vacuum cleaner, or placing your golf ball on the tee, use the correct, easy, protective Boutelle bending down action. I call this Dustpan-and-Brush; try it now, preferably in front of your desk, bureau, counter or other support at first until you gain easy balance and don't need any support:

1. Stand in correct alignment (Chapter III). Breathe rhythmically throughout this natural-action, remembering to *exhale* as you go down, and *inhale* as you lift. Step straight forward a few inches with your right foot, left heel leaving the floor slightly, so that your body is supported in a strong stance, most of your weight on the balls of your feet . . .

2a: Place your fingertips on the edge of a table or other support, keeping your elbows flexed and close (but not tight) to the sides of your body, not spread out. Look straight ahead and slowly bend your knees forward in alignment with your feet until you are resting close to the floor, no straining. 2b: Release your hands and place them aligned at your sides, fingers relaxed and pointing toward the floor. Keep back straight, think IN, think UP—as you rest in this position and breathe rhythmically, easily . . .

3. *Exhale* as you place your fingertips on the edge of your support . . . keeping elbows flexed and close to your sides . . . push back on

1

2A

2B

your left heel . . . slowly rise to standing position. Bring your right foot back even with your left, arms back to your sides in original standing alignment.

Then practice this natural-action beginning with your left foot forward. When you can accomplish the action easily in front of your support with either foot forward, try it with a dustpan and brush, or any other stooping task. You are using your pelvic, thigh and lower leg muscles correctly, never putting undue stress on your lower back muscles. Your shoulders and body will be relaxed and supported without strain, and you are avoiding trouble by going down grace-fully with knees flexed and in alignment, instead of bending and angling your body dangerously.

ELBOWS-IN ALWAYS FOR PUSH-PULL AND OVERHEAD ACTIONS

Please read every word of these elbows-in instructions carefully to help avoid the pain and grief of "shoulder flare-up," "tennis elbow," and other arm muscle troubles that not only beset tennis players, but also houseworkers, window washers, teachers, and others who use their arms a good deal. For trouble-free performance, don't treat your poor elbows as abused hinges that you hang out like air-liner wings; instead, keep them in correct alignment and close (not tight) to your sides as you perform daily tasks. Remind yourself con-stantly until it becomes part of you to *keep elbows in* when styling your hair, wiping walls and countertops, washing windows, wiping a windshield, pushing a vacuum cleaner, baby carriage or lawn mower, typing, sewing, riding a bicycle, many other common ac-tions. It isn't the activity that causes problems, it's doing it wrong—so don't flap your elbows out like a baby bird in flight!

Push-Pull Actions with the arms must be done with elbows in correct alignment close to the body, as in A-8 Rowing Action (Chapter VII), with elbows performing a forward-and-back, natural hinge-type action (practice A-8 now in standing position).

Review M-6 Upper Joints Mobilizer (Chapter IX) for correct arm

and elbow actions in and out from the sides of the body, as in sweeping with a broom (practice M-6 now).

Check and practice the correct action of the elbows in A-9, The Wave (Chapter VII).

For synchronized control of arm, elbow and shoulder in daily tasks, practice and master B-12 Tailor Sit Pendulum Swing (Chapter VIII), with special benefits for racquet-sports enthusiasts.

Overhead Reach Actions such as pulling down shades, reaching high shelves, and wiping high places must be performed with the elbow maintaining alignment with the side of the body. Practice this basic correcting and conditioning action:

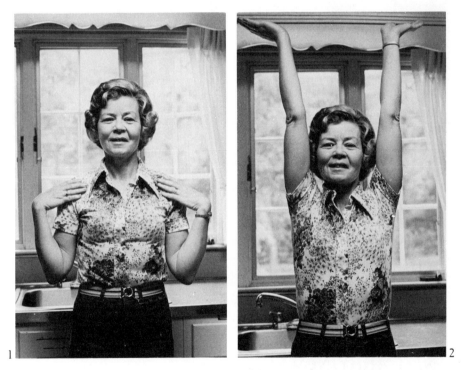

1. Stand in correct alignment. Flex your elbows and press them against your sides, then place your hands on your shoulder caps . . .

2a: Now flex your wrists out so that your fingers are facing away from your body. 2b: *Exhale* and push your arms straight upward over your shoulder joints as if you were balancing an egg on each outstretched hand. 2c: When your arms are fully extended, elbow joints locked, stretch your fingers straight up toward the ceiling . . .

2   3

3. Flex your wrists so fingers face toward your body, and return smoothly to starting position.

Repeat entire action *five times* to condition and strengthen your arm and hand muscles, to improve flexibility of shoulder, elbow, wrist and finger joints, to promote proper alignment in performing overhead-reach tasks properly, and to help avoid injury and pain.

RULES FOR LIFTING AND CARRYING OBJECTS

Many back injuries and other troubles are brought on or aggravated by lifting and carrying weighty objects improperly. It is always important in lifting to *flex the knees properly* as instructed, and to *keep elbows in* when carrying. Observe these additional rules:

1: Never try to lift and carry more than one-quarter of your weight by yourself.

2a: Lift by flexing your knees and exerting your leg and pelvic muscles rather than lower back muscles . . . 2b: and keep elbows in when lifting and carrying objects, thus relieving shoulder and arm muscles and joints.

3: Carry a heavy object in *front* of your pelvis, using both hands, elbows in, legs in correct alignment.

4: In lifting and carrying a heavy object, balance it against your thigh and other muscle areas, never on elbow, shoulder, hip, or knee joints.

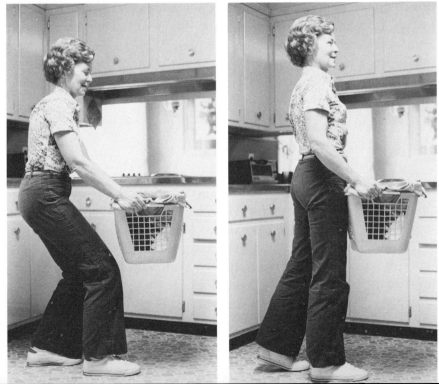

PUTTING YOUR BEST FEET FORWARD

In your daily living actions, you are on your feet much of the day, so I can't understand why practically all other "fitness programs" neglect them. If your feet don't support you properly, you are in trouble, and "when your feet hurt, you hurt all over." It's an essential part of the Boutelle Method to condition ankles and feet in your "A" and "B" programs, along with the special, simple natural-actions here—to strengthen ankles and feet, provide relief from tired feet and tight ankles, and help prevent many problems. Please note these brief points:

• *Ligaments of the feet must be pliant and flexible,* since a network of these straplike bands of tough, fibrous tissue supports the mass of interrelated foot bones and provides maximum freedom of movement. You must counteract the negative effect of much "stylish" footwear which inhibits and weakens the foot's natural free movements.

• *Maintaining maximum flexibility of ankle joints* is necessary not only to provide firm body support, but also to help prevent ankle sprains, which are today's most common injury. The ankle is a *hinge-like* joint which permits flexion (bending) and extension but not complete rotation. You must remember to place your feet a few inches apart (as stressed throughout this book) so that your ankle joints are in proper alignment under your hip joints, to help prevent undue stress on the ligaments that keep the ankle joint in position.

The following special "F" ("Foot") natural-actions strengthen feet and ankles and provide wanted relief quickly.

F-1 FOOT-ANKLE ACTIVATOR

1. Sit on the floor with legs extended straight forward, a few inches apart in ankle-hip alignment, toes pointed forward, back straight up . . . straight arms extended to sides, aligned with hip sockets, fingertips touching the floor . . . *exhale (blow!)* . . .

2. Now *inhale deeply* as you flex your ankles so that your heels round up and leave the floor slightly, and your toes point back toward your body . . . keeping knees locked . . .

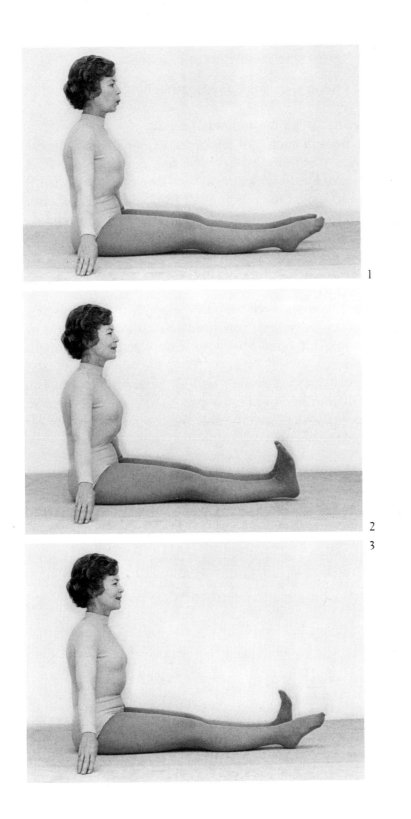

1

2

3

Exhale as you extend your ankle joints, stretching toes forward as in 1.

Repeat this flexing-stretching action *ten times* . . .

3. Now alternate with each foot *ten times*, one foot flexing as the other is extending, rhythmically. Feel the fine conditioning effect through your feet, ankles, and leg muscles. (Don't be concerned if your heels refuse to leave the floor at all at first—they will do better day after day as your ankles regain full natural flexing-extending ability.)

F-2 TARSAL FLEXOR

The tarsals are the joints, with supporting ligaments and muscles, which enable you to move your feet from side to side and forward and back, simulating rotation. This easy natural-action is a superb flexing conditioner.

1a. In the same beginning position as F-1 . . . *exhale* as you push into the floor with your heels as if gluing them in place (but keeping legs straight, knees locked) . . . 1b. and rotate your feet *outward*, reaching for the floor with each little toe, separating your toes wide . . .

2. *Inhale* as you rotate feet *inward* until toes of right foot cross over left foot toes, curling your toes in during this action.

Repeat this outward-and-inward complete action *ten times*, alter-

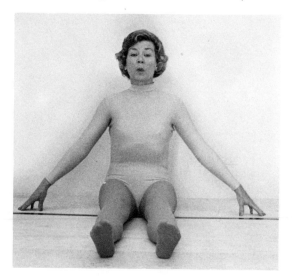

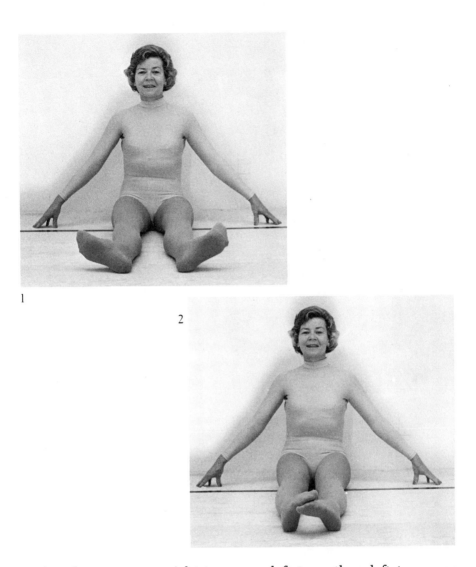

1

2

nating the toe cross—right toes over left toes, then left toes over right toes.

F-3 PLANTAR PIVOT

This is an excellent natural-action for tired feet, flat feet, and fallen arches. I sometimes call it "Snap-Crackle" if you hear ankle-bones gliding one against the other. Throughout, the vulnerable ankle joints are held in support—never force or overstrain, keep movements smooth. *Inhale and exhale deeply* at your natural pace.

1. Sit in correct alignment in a straight chair, bare or stockinged

1 2A   2B

2C

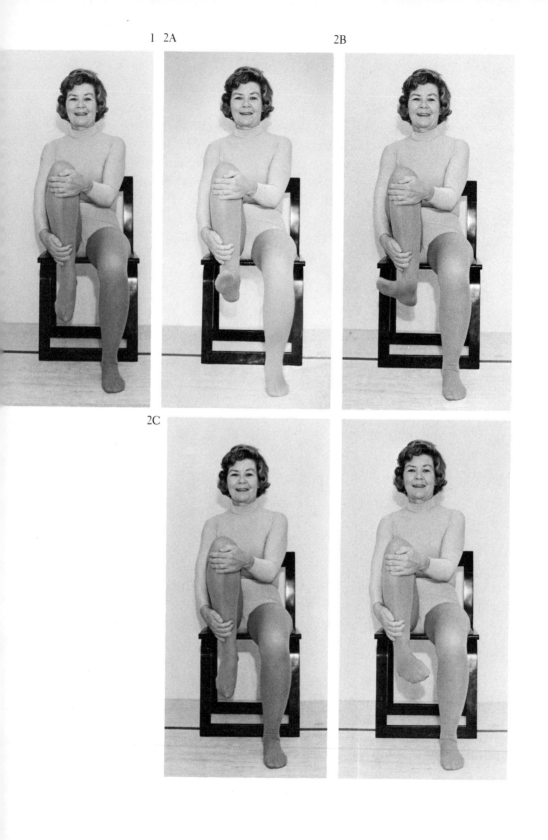

feet. Move slightly forward toward the edge of the seat . . . clasp your right knee with your left hand . . . and lift your right leg until you can wrap your right hand firmly around the outside of your right ankle. Keep your pectoral pins IN, no slumping shoulders . . .

2a. Flex your right foot so that the sole (plantar) surface is facing forward . . . 2b. and gently rotate the ball of the foot outward . . . 2c. down . . . inward . . . and up to starting position.

Rotate *five times* slowly . . . then change to left foot and repeat *five times*.

This entire series of special natural-actions takes only a few minutes, and has a superb relieving, conditioning effect. I urge you to perform them all once or twice a day when convenient for you, and whenever you need quick relief from tired or aching feet.

STANDING-TO-SITTING: THE BOUTELLE PELVIC PUTDOWN

Just angling, slouching, or collapsing into a seat from a standing position can be injurious as well as awkward-looking. Practice this smooth, no-strain Boutelle "pelvic putdown," then make it part of your graceful movements.

1. Stand in correct alignment with your back a few inches in front of the chair. Think IN, think UP, back straight.

2. *Inhale* as you flex your knees and put your sitting bones down, maintaining correct alignment—not angling body to the side, backward or forward.

3. Your pelvis will move into proper sitting position smoothly as your shoulders remain quiet and relaxed, not slumping or hunching.

4. To return to standing position, make sure first that your ankle joints are aligned a few inches apart under your knee joints. *Exhale* as you move your erect upper body slightly forward toward your knees (never slumping) and lift your sitting bones from your seat, thus arising smoothly and gracefully.

When sitting, make sure that you have "hand clearance" (about an inch) between the edge of the seat and the backs of your knees.

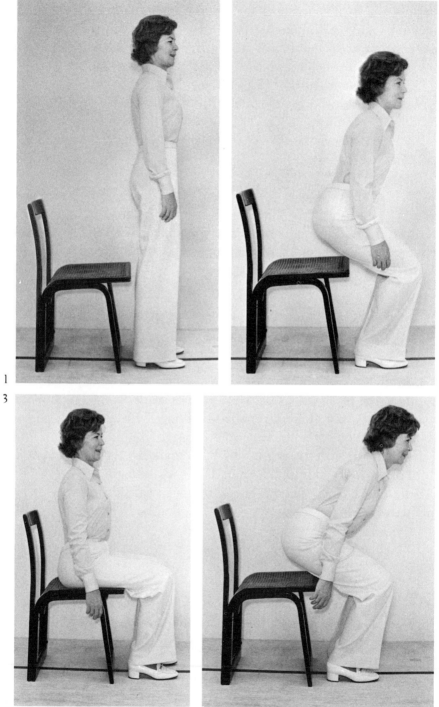

1

2

3

4

Check by placing flattened hand behind your knee; the top edge of your hand should reach slightly higher than the seat. Be careful not to let the backs of your knees press tightly against the edge of a seat as this can interfere with circulation in your legs.

BOUTELLE ANALYTICAL WALKING

Please analyze yourself for the following common errors in walking. I warn my classes that we have become a world of *knee pushers*—instead of walking with a smooth, springy stride from the ball-and-socket *hip joint*. Like too many people, do you walk with your shoulders hunched forward, pushing each foot ahead with your vulnerable knee joints? Or, in walking, do you push one knee toward or against the other incorrectly, as so many do? (No wonder "housemaid's knee"—chronic inflammation, pain, swelling—is a common

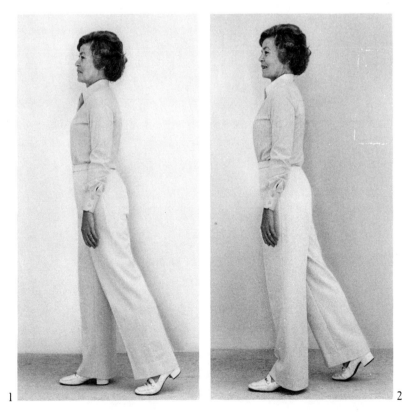

1   2

affliction!) Instead, from now on, move smoothly, naturally, gracefully by practicing the following analytical walking action:

1. Think IN, think UP throughout—stretch your right leg forward from your right hip *socket* . . . letting the heel gently touch the ground first and then pushing your weight forward onto the ball of your right foot. Keep your right shoulder, hip and knee in correct alignment over your right foot, which points straight ahead, not inward or outward . . .

2. Now stretch your left leg forward from your left hip socket, transferring your weight lightly onto your left heel and then fully to the ball of your left foot. Concentrate on your hip sockets (not your knees) doing the walking, evenly aligned with each step.

Practice the following *five times:* Take four steps forward, followed by four steps backward in correct alignment—thinking IN, thinking UP always. Remember to keep feet pointed straight forward.

SMOOTH SIDE STEP

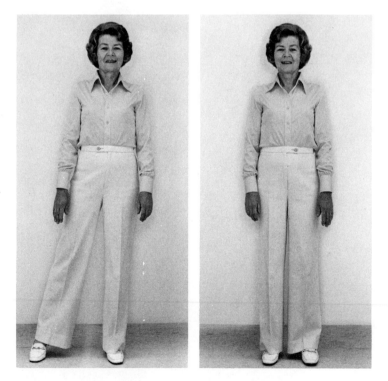

In the course of a day's movements, you often step to the side. It's important to sidestep in correct alignment for easy, graceful, no-strain functioning, not pushing or forcing with your knees, but using your hip sockets properly in this way:

1. Stand in correct alignment . . . then place your right leg straight out to the right side from your hip socket . . . shifting your weight onto the ball of your right foot . . .

2. Now, from your left hip socket, draw your left leg into aligned position under your left hip socket. Note that you are flexing your ankle rather than your knee.

Practice by sidestepping four steps to the right, then four steps to the left, *five times*. With correct side-stepping, you will improve your grace and balance and have better control, especially on slippery and steep surfaces.

CLIMBING STAIRS

Most people climb stairs incorrectly—swaying, bending, slouching, putting undue stress on joints and strain on muscles. Here are the simple tips for climbing easily, gracefully, with least effort:

• Think IN, think UP every step of the way, keeping your body upright, thereby maintaining best body support as you climb or descend steps.

• Check your basic head-shoulder-hip-knee-ankle alignment in climbing, as in standing or walking properly . . . as you push forward onto the ball of each ascending foot. This correct alignment helps keep joints and muscles from twisting, weakening, and possibly incurring damage. Keep feet pointed straight forward.

• If you become at all winded or tired, *stop*, stand in correct alignment with extra support from hand on banister or wall if necessary, and rest before continuing. While resting, practice rhythmic breathing slowly—breathe in deeply, blow out forcefully—at least *three times*.

AUTOMOBILE NATURAL-ACTIONS

If you are a driver, you have probably said on the phone, "I'll jump into the car and be right over." That's all wrong! Never "jump into" or slump or slouch into your car, thus inviting injury. Instead, take it easy—stop for an instant after opening the door, and put yourself into the car smoothly and gracefully with this "Boutelle auto pelvic putdown":

1. Step in from the side with your right foot, right knee and right hip in alignment, not twisting or jerking your body into the car. Put your pelvis down slowly until you are well supported on your sitting bones . . . then draw your left leg into the car, and place your left foot down in alignment with your left knee and hip. Close the door, and place your hands on the wheel with your elbows flexed in alignment with your sides, not poking outward like open wings . . .

2. Now think IN, think UP as you settle firmly on your sitting bones—you are sitting TALL. Adjust the rear view mirror for full visibility. Fasten your seat belt. Breathe rhythmically . . . start the motor . . . release the brake . . . and you are on your way, your car and you "running smooth."

As you drive, if you find you have to adjust your mirror for full visibility, that's a signal that your body has slumped. Instead of mov-

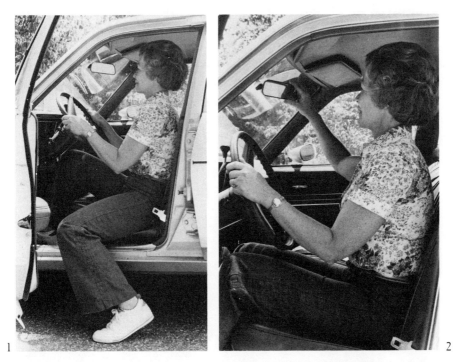

1   2

ing the mirror, adjust your posture again to the think IN, think UP, sitting TALL position. Keep your elbows in IN position, in alignment with the sides of your body. Letting your elbows spread out tends to throw your body and back out of alignment, and puts undue stress on arm muscles and back, draining energy.

Don't drive with one hand on top of the wheel and an elbow resting on or outside a window ledge. That's a hazard not only to your driving safety, but to your *shoulder girdle muscles* as well.

As a passenger in a car, bus, airplane, or other transport, sit in proper alignment always—feet and knees a few inches apart in alignment with your hips. Sit solidly on your sitting bones—think IN, think UP, sit TALL. Don't let the backs of your knees press against the edge of the seat, since that may interfere with leg circulation. Incorrect sitting, sagging, slumping or twisting throw your body out of alignment and invite back and muscle trouble and fatigue.

When sitting for a long time in a bus, plane, office chair, or elsewhere, here are two simple natural-actions that will help relieve sitting strain and provide a quick pick-up.

SITTING PULL-UP

1. Grasp the bottom of the seat (both sides preferably) with your hands . . . elbows and arms in alignment with your sides. *Inhale* as you pull your upper body up from your hips to the top of your head, as though a rope attached to the top of your head is pulling you upward. Think IN (abdomen in), think UP (chest and shoulders), pushpins IN, chin zipped UP at right angle to your neck.

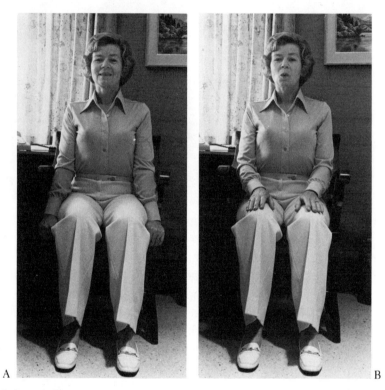

A   B

2. Hold the pull-up position a few seconds . . . then *blow like a whale* as you relax your arms and upper body, and rest hands on thighs, but without slumping or letting your back touch the back of the seat. Repeat entire action slowly *five times*.

KNEE PUMP

1. Without holding seat . . . arms relaxed at your sides . . . your back not touching the back of the seat . . . think IN, think UP . . .

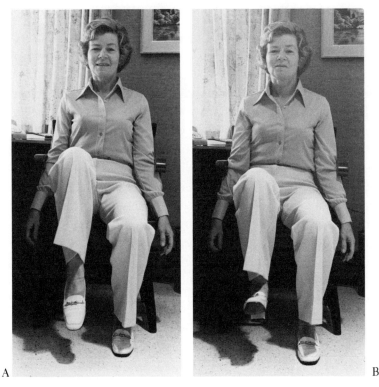

A   B

breathe in and out deeply and rhythmically as you slowly pump up your right and left knees and legs alternately from the floor . . . lifting each leg, in turn, a few inches from the floor (right leg up, then down as left leg pulls up, and so on).

  2. As each leg rises, point toes downward, then flex ankle as you lower leg to rest foot flat on the floor again. Repeat, lifting and dropping each leg *five times* for a total of *ten times*.

ADDITIONAL DAILY-ACTION REMINDERS

• *Make correct standing, walking, and sitting alignment* a natural part of your daily activities by checking your alignment occasionally all day long . . . while brushing your teeth, stand correctly, keep elbow IN . . . check when passing or facing a mirror, when catching your reflection in a store window, every time you enter a room, while seated at desk or table as you work or eat.

• *Concentrate on "think IN, think UP"* when working at desk or elsewhere . . . standing at a checkout counter . . . sitting at meetings or social gatherings . . . watching TV . . . and in all other standard everyday actions and positions.

• *Practice slow, deep, rhythmic breathing* as a special natural-action a number of times during the day—at your desk or table—and especially for release of tension whenever you may feel uptight, frustrated, pressured, depressed. You're bound to gain some relief emotionally, and you'll feel better physically as you breathe in, *blow out*—slowly, deeply, rhythmically—clearing out carbon dioxide, bringing in revivifying fresh air right to the bottom of your lungs.

• *Reminder: Run smooth in everything you do* throughout your waking hours. Avoid jerking, wrenching, sudden push and pull, extreme stretching, exerting instead of resting a moment or more when you feel exhausted . . . and bending, reaching, and lifting except in the graceful, coordinated Boutelle natural-actions as instructed.

XI

Special Natural-Actions to Improve Sports Abilities

The primary lesson every sports participant has to learn is this: *You must get into condition to play a sport, rather than use a sport to get into condition!* Your good health and total performance depend on your *total conditioning*, not just on how you stroke or swing or stride; ask any sports champion. You can take hundreds of lessons from a top pro in your particular sport—tennis, golf, whatever—but you can't possibly achieve your best possible score unless your entire body is conditioned for needed muscle tone, balance, coordination, and endurance.

Furthermore, be warned by the fact that the sports boom has also brought about shocking increases in the number of injured sports enthusiasts in the waiting rooms of many physicians and orthopedic surgeons. There is absolutely no question that if your body is well conditioned inside-out, *you are less prone to injury*. When your body isn't ready for increased activity, and you engage in tennis, skiing, softball, running, or other active sports and recreation, you are inviting mishaps, pain, and possibly permanent injury.

Even if you are experienced at a sport, when you go back into action after a layoff, and are not in top condition, you can suffer "neuromuscular lag." That is, your *mind* may remember what to do, and *tell* your body how to perform, but your reaction time has slowed down and you cannot perform properly. The result too often is strain, pain, and damage—perhaps serious and sometimes permanent. The same applies to the "weekend" and "vacation athlete." Your daily Boutelle session is necessary to put you in good condition and keep you in your top form for both everyday and sports activities.

IMPROVING YOUR COORDINATION

Later in this chapter are selected natural-actions for specific sports. In addition, here are special, essential actions recommended for improving your balance and coordination, as well as muscle tone. Lack of coordination can keep you from performing at your best and can lead to mishaps even if your muscle tone is excellent. *Coordination* is well defined as "the coordinated functioning of muscles in the execution of a complex task . . . harmonizing [all elements] in a common action."

The following "S" (for "Sports") natural-actions are designed to improve the basic coordination needed for most recreational sports.

S-1   HIP-HEIGHT ARM COORDINATOR

1. Stand in correct alignment; place your palms on the fronts of your thighs. *Exhale* as you bend your knees about halfway down, not a deep full knee bend . . .

2. *Inhale* as you slowly straighten your knees and legs to standing position, and *at the same time* raise your right arm *forward* to hip height . . . and your left arm to the *side* in line with and no higher than your left hip . . . then, holding the positions of your arms, and keeping your shoulder muscles motionless, give an extra *stretch* into space with your fingertips . . .

3. *Exhale* as you return your hands to the starting position on fronts of thighs . . . *at the same time* bend your knees again . . .

4. Now repeat action 1 . . . but this time pushing left arm forward and right arm to the side . . . then return to starting position.

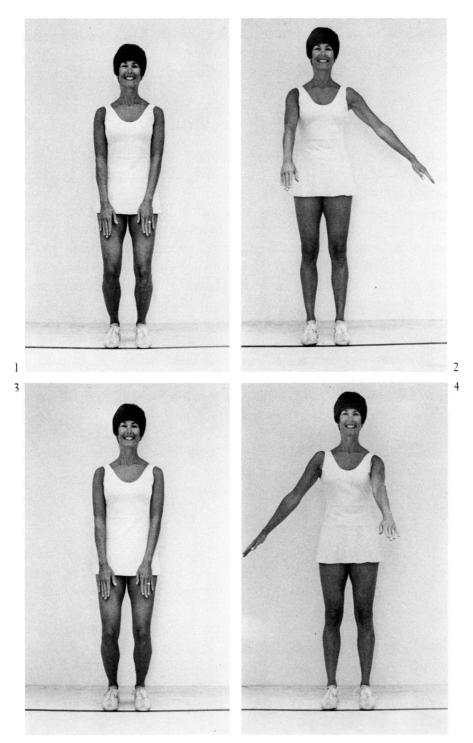

1

2

3

4

Alternating actions 1 and 3, repeat *five times* each. With each action, say to yourself as you move in a smooth flow:

2 and 4: *Inhale . . . pull up . . . stretch . . .*
3: *Exhale . . . push down . . . knee bend . . .*

S-2   OVERHEAD ARM COORDINATOR

1. Stand in correct alignment . . . stretch straight arms high over your shoulder joints, palms facing each other, fingertips reaching toward ceiling . . . *inhale* . . .

2a. *Blow out* as you rotate your whole arms so that your *right* palm faces forward, and *left* palm faces left . . . in continuing action, flex wrists downward as you bend knees slowly halfway to the floor . . . (2b) and push right arm forward and down to hip height, left arm to side and down to hip height . . . pushing firmly with heels of your hands, and keeping elbows locked . . .

3. *Inhale* as you rotate whole arms so palms face up . . . slowly straightening your knees and legs . . . leading with heels of hands as straight arms move up and return to starting position.

Repeat entire actions, this time with *left* palm facing forward, and *right* palm facing right . . . left arm moving forward, and right arm to right side. Repeat alternating arm actions *five times* . . . saying to yourself:

2a, 2b: *Exhale . . . knee-bend . . . push . . .*
3: *Inhale . . . pull-up . . . stretch . . .*

S-3   LEG COORDINATOR

1. Stand in correct alignment, arms at sides . . . *exhale* as you bend knees halfway down (not deep knee bend) . . . keeping feet in alignment with respective hip joints throughout, whether feet are on the floor or in the air . . .

2. *Inhale* as you straighten *left* knee and leg . . . and *at same time* lift *right* leg with knee flexed so upper leg is at right angle to body at hip height . . . balancing body with weight on left leg . . .

3. *Exhale* as you return legs to starting position with both legs in modified knee bend . . .

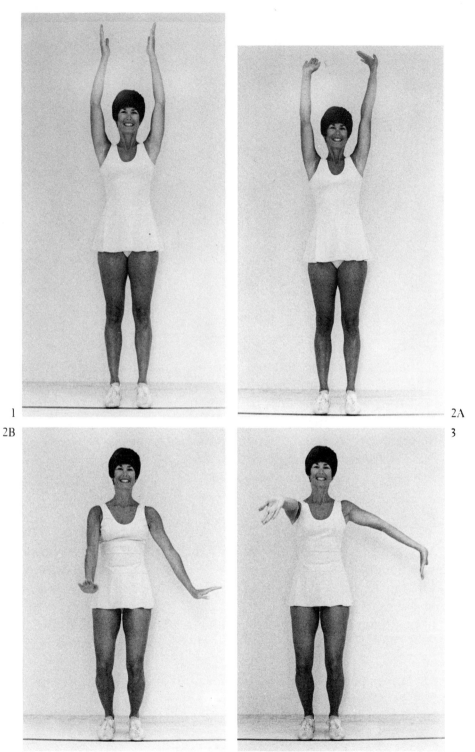

1

2A

2B

3

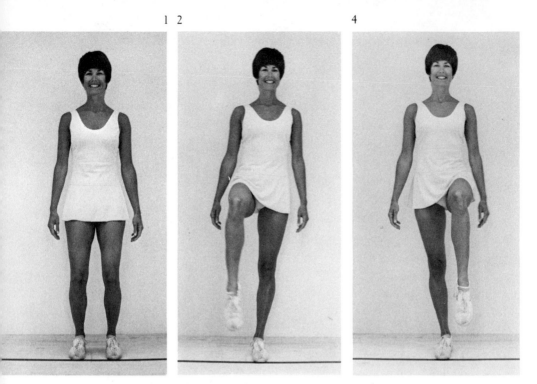

4. *Inhale* and repeat action 1, but this time straighten *right* leg and flex *left* knee up to hip height, balancing body with all weight on right leg . . . then return to position 2 . . . keeping all actions flowing in slow, continuous motion.

Repeat entire alternating actions *five times*, saying to yourself:

2 and 4: *Inhale . . . straighten . . . flex . . .*

3: *Exhale . . . return . . . knee-bend . . .*

S-4 LEG-ARM-HIP COORDINATOR

Be sure to master S-1, S-2, and S-3 thoroughly before you tackle this "ultimate" coordinator, which will promote your total harmonious functioning to improve your timing and performance remarkably.

1. Stand in correct alignment, then place your palms on fronts of your thighs . . . *Inhale* as you flex both knees in a modified knee bend . . .

2a: Move your straight *right* arm forward, and straight *left* arm to the left side, both at hip height . . .

2b: *Exhale* as you straighten your *right* leg . . . and lift *left* leg with flexed knee rising to hip height . . . weight resting on right leg . . .

3a: *Inhale* and return to starting position with palms on fronts of thighs . . . flex knees . . . move straight *left* arm forward, and straight *right* arm to right side, both at hip height . . .

3b: *Exhale* as you straighten *left* leg . . . and lift *right* leg with flexed knee rising to hip height . . . weight resting on left leg . . . then *inhale* as you return to starting position.

Repeat entire alternating actions *five times* saying to yourself as actions flow:

1 and 3a: *Inhale . . . knee-bend . . . stretch . . .*
2b and 3b: *Exhale . . . exchange-lift . . .*

When you become fully proficient at S-4, which is a very challenging series of natural-action coordinators, try adding a *hop* to the supporting foot . . . and now you will say to yourself:

1 and 3a: *Inhale . . . knee-bend . . . stretch . . .*
2 and 4: *Exhale . . . exchange-lift . . . HOP . . .*

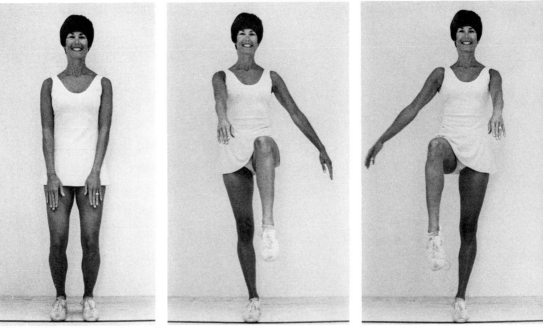

1   2A-2B   3A-3B

With practice, you will be increasing your cardiovascular endurance measurably. As you conquer all these coordinators, you can gradually speed up the actions and increase the number of repetitions. You will be on your way to becoming a superstar indeed! However, the basic Boutelle cautions remain, as always: Don't overstrain . . . don't overtrain . . . if you ever feel overtired and/or trembly, *stop and rest*.

S-5 FOREARM STRENGTHENER

This is a super, anytime conditioner for the tennis and paddle enthusiast, golfer, bowler—anyone who needs to strengthen the *extensor* and *supinator* forearm muscles. These muscles should be in top condition for the follow-through swinging actions involved in these and other sports. Try it standing, sitting, watching TV, listening to music—whenever most convenient for you.

1. Extend your straight arms forward, wrists in line with hip sockets, elbows locked, palms up . . . fingers curled into tight fists . . . *exhale* . . .

2a: *Inhale* as you flex your elbows, keeping palms up, drawing

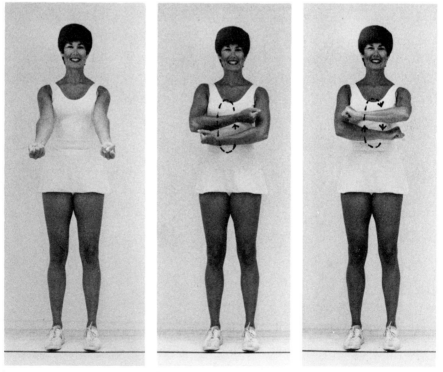

1   2A-2B   3A-3B

your right forearm across front of chest but not touching your body . . . and draw your left forearm in front of right forearm . . .

2b: *Exhale* (blow like a whale!) as you roll right forearm up and over left forearm . . . and left forearm under and over right forearm (forearms not quite touching chest). Keep your elbows *stationary* as you continue this double rolling action smoothly, speedily—*counting five* . . .

3a: Stop . . . *Inhale* as you rotate both forearms so palms (fists still clenched) now face *down* . . .

3b: *Exhale* deeply, fully, as you *reverse* the rolling action . . . right forearm rolling under and over as left forearm rolls up and over. Remember to keep elbows in a stationary position as you *count five* . . .

4: Stop . . . *inhale* as you rotate forearms so palms (fists still clenched) again face *up* . . . as in 2a . . .

5: *Exhale* as you release arms and extend them to starting position.

Repeat entire action *three times*, a few times daily, but never overstraining. You'll find this a remarkably effective forearm strengthener which should improve your sports ability as it has for so many Boutelle sports enthusiasts.

For quicker results, you may perform your entire coordination session several times a day if you wish—but remember, don't overstrain, ever.

SELECTED NATURAL-ACTIONS FOR SPECIFIC POPULAR SPORTS

I must emphasize again to enthusiastic sports participants the need for the basic all-over neuromuscular conditioning you get from your regular daily Boutelle sessions—don't skip them, no matter how active you are in sports. In the following listing, as an addition to the special sports actions, I have selected standard natural-actions particularly to help improve your performance in your favorite sports activity. In doing these natural-actions daily, simply increase the number of repetitions and speed up the actions gradually—but never to the point of strain or exhaustion. No matter what, remember to *run smooth* as you perform the stepped-up actions ("A" actions are in Chapter VII., "B" actions are in Chapter VIII., "M" actions are in Chapter IX):

BICYCLING: A-2, A-3, A-5, A-6, A-11, A-12, B-2, B-3, B-6, B-8, B-10, B-11.

BOWLING: A-1, A-4, A-8, A-9, A-10, A-12, B-1, B-7, B-9, B-12, M-6.

GOLF: A-3, A-5, A-6, A-9, A-12, B-2, B-3, B-5, B-9, B-12.

SKATING: A-5, A-6, A-11, A-12, B-2, B-3, B-4, B-6, B-9, B-11, B-12, Smooth Sidestep (Chapter X).

SKIING: Same as for skating; add Tennis Swing Breathing (Chapter IV).

SWIMMING: A-5, A-6, A-7, A-8, A-9, A-11, B-2, B-3, B-4, B-5, B-6, B-7, B-12.

TENNIS & PADDLE: A-5, A-6, A-9, A-11, A-12, B-2, B-3, B-6, B-7, B-9, B-12, M-6, Smooth Sidestep (Chapter X) . . . Tennis Swing Breathing (Chapter IV).

XII
Special Natural-Actions to Trim "Problem Spots"

When referring to body "problem spots," most women mean (1) bulging or loose midsection areas of abdomen, waistline, hips, buttocks; (2) flabby thighs; or (3) loose upper arms. "Trimming" actually is a result of firming those areas *in conjunction with conditioning your body all over and inside-out*. Don't believe anyone who tells you that doing a few isolated movements can trim problem spots. Your regular Boutelle "A" and "B" programs have a trimming-firming effect by conditioning all 632 muscles and all parts of your body day after day. But don't fool yourself that doing only so-called "trimming exercises," as some advocate, will work. It won't!

Well-conditioned muscles all over hold bones in place properly, and interact most efficiently to help us lift, twist, turn, and move most effectively and smoothly. If, however, abdominal muscles are weak, midsection areas bulge and droop through lack of support (as well as from overweight in some cases). If pelvic muscles are flabby, they are like loose garters that don't hold leg muscles well, resulting in loose thighs. Similarly, it takes firm shoulder girdle muscles to help keep upper arms from being flabby.

Realize that *every* natural-action has a coordinated firming effect as you condition your body all over in your daily "A" or "B" program. For extra firming-trimming effect on problem spots, I recommend a *second* session each day of certain selected natural-actions, plus the added special trimming conditioners provided. With all of them, and with your daily "A" or "B" program, note the firming-trimming effect as you move through each session—without forcing, jerking, overstraining—performing always with your torso, arms and legs in correct alignment. Measuring with a tape measure will convince you of the dimension-trimming effectiveness week after week as you beautify your body and improve your grace, balance, and coordination.

In your *second* firming-trimming session each day, perform the following selected "A" and "B" natural-actions—*plus* the special "P" (for "Problem Spots") natural-actions (but don't do the "B" actions below until you are in the "B" program).

Note: "A" actions are in Chapter VII, "B" actions are in Chapter VIII.

MIDSECTION (Abdomen, waist, hips, buttocks): A-1, A-4, B-5.
ARMS (especially flabby upper arms): A-8, B-7, B-12.
THIGHS (especially inner thighs, legs): A-11, B-4, B-6.

P-1   STRIDE-SLIDE MIDSECTION TRIMMER

This fine natural-action firms the hips, waistline, insides of thighs, arms. Think IN, think UP, keep your pectoral pins IN throughout.

1. Begin in a long-sit position as in A-8 (Chapter VII) . . . rotate your entire legs so that your toes face out (away from body) . . . and push legs open to a comfortable wide stride position . . . arms behind you so that your hands overlap near the base of your spine . . .

2. Keep your left arm behind you, but stretch your extended *right* arm along the inside of your right leg (without bending your neck) . . . and *gently* turn your neck to focus your eyes over your left shoulder . . .

3. In this position, slide your upper body *forward and back smoothly*, arm guiding and sliding along the inside of your right leg . . . moving from your hip sockets, keeping back straight, no bending or slumping. *Exhale* (blow out!) as you slide forward . . . *inhale* deeply as you slide back.

Slide forward and back *three times* . . . then lift back to starting position. Now repeat sliding actions with right arm behind you, and left arm doing the guiding along inside of left leg—*three times*. Feel the trimming pull in your waistline, thighs, and arms as you slide smoothly, pectoral pins IN.

As you proceed day after day, you can gradually spread your straight legs apart wider, increasing stretch of the sliding-firming action, but never overstraining.

P-2 ADVANCED STRIDE-STRETCH

This progressed natural-action should be done only after you are in the "B" Best program (Chapter VIII). It's excellent for firming-trimming your midsection, thighs, lower legs, arms.

1. Take the stride position as in P-1 . . . straight legs as wide apart as comfortable, but with ankles flexed so feet point upward.

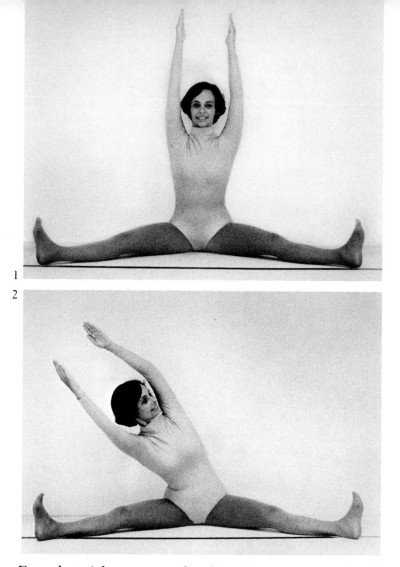

1

2

Extend straight arms overhead in alignment over shoulders, palms facing in . . .

2. *Inhale* . . . as you turn your upper torso to the *left* (keeping your pectoral pins IN throughout, no slumping of shoulders, not letting your overhead arms fall forward) . . . and *exhale* as you stretch your upper torso over your *right* leg in a sliding motion, reaching as far forward as possible without overstraining . . .

Inhale . . . as you return to starting position . . . then repeat the stretching-sliding slowly, rhythmically, *three times* . . .

Now repeat the same total action *three times*, but stretch your upper torso to the *right* . . . as you do the stretching-sliding action forward and over your *left* leg.

P-3 THIGH-TRIMMER PUSHUP

This natural-action is very effective for firming and trimming mid-section and especially conditioning upper thigh muscles as well as lower leg muscles.

1. Start by lying face down on the floor . . . ankles and knees in alignment with hip sockets . . . toes pointed back . . . elbows flexed . . . right palm over left palm, placed directly under chin, your forehead resting comfortably on your hands . . . flexed arms forming a straight line across from one elbow to the other . . .

2. *Inhale* as you flex your knees and draw your lower legs up over your sitting muscles (gluteals) with toes pointing up toward ceiling . . . feet as close to your buttocks as possible without straining . . . thighs remaining against the floor . . .

3. *Exhale* as you stretch your legs back to starting position, but place the *balls* of your toes on the floor, heels up. Throughout, think IN, keep your abdomen tight against the floor . . .

4. *Inhale* and push your straight legs upward, knees locked, so that your thighs leave the floor a little, weight on the balls of your feet . . . keeping your abdomen on the floor in holding position.

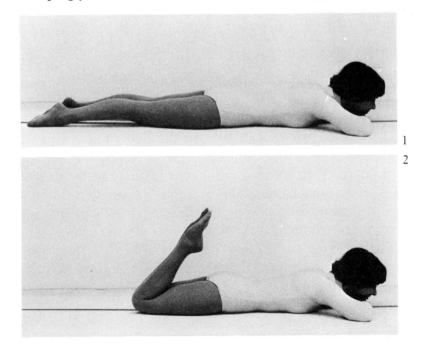

1

2

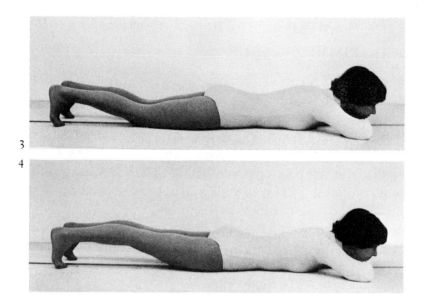

3

4

5. *Exhale* and flex your knees slightly to place your upper thighs on the floor . . . and stretch your lower legs and feet in returning to the starting position.

Repeat five times, feeling the firming effect in your thighs and lower legs as you move slowly and rhythmically through these very effective actions.

P-4 BOUTELLE OBLIQUE TWIST

This super natural-action especially firms the "handlebar muscles," the *obliques* of the waistline (to be done only after you are in the "B" Best program).

1. Start by lying face down on the floor, flexed elbows directly under shoulders, lower arms and palms resting on the floor. Bring your rib cage off the floor, and your head up with ears over shoulders. Keep your hands and lower arms flat on floor throughout . . .

2. *Inhale* as you flex your left knee and draw your left lower leg up over your left hip . . .

3. *Exhale* as you lift your left thigh and left hip and twist to your *right* side without overstraining, pushing your left toes toward the floor . . . your elbows and forearms remaining down in a resting position . . .

4. *Inhale* as you return to position 2 . . .

5. *Exhale* as you place your left hip and left thigh on the floor, and stretch your lower leg back to original starting position.

Perform the same series of actions but starting with your *right* leg . . . and complete *five times* with each leg, total of *ten times* in all.

Concentrate on keeping your pectoral pins IN when performing this splendid firming-trimming action, thus preventing tension buildup in your shoulder girdle muscles. *Run smooth* as you master this demanding natural-action—don't overstrain at any point.

1

2

3

XIII

For Men Only:
Male Boutelle Program for Lifetime Fitness

Dear Sir: Please read the brief but extremely important opening chapters of this book carefully to understand fully how the unique, basic principles of the Boutelle Method can help you personally to attain and maintain your maximum fitness now and for your lifetime. Note the specific, special benefits of this all-over inside-out *neuromuscular* (nerve and muscle) conditioning, as contrasted with outmoded "exercise" and "calisthenics" programs. Realize that the best present you can give yourself and your loved ones is to take care of yourself and become the best you can be in every way.

Boutelle *natural-action* conditioning is adapted for you in this section, as in my "His and Her" classes, taking into account fundamental male/female anatomical differences. Like many men, including physicians who participate and who recommend both male and female patients to my classes, you can improve your working, recreational, and sports performance remarkably. You can become a more proficient and *safer* "weekend athlete," with superior coordination and muscle *tonus* (elasticity), leading to stepped-up energy and stamina. (Be sure to read and use Chapter XI on improving sports abilities.)

You will learn how to "think IN, think UP" . . . keep your "pectoral pins" IN . . . sit, stand, walk, move in smooth, healthful, correct *Boutelle alignment* always. You will gain the benefits of *rhythmic-flow breathing* as you "blow like a whale!" . . . and get needed vitality boosts with the quick "neuromuscular anytime energizers."

As a test beginning, turn back to Chapter V and try the two quick energizers right now, however you are dressed. (You can even do the first one easily and inobtrusively while seated in your office, living room, or anywhere—simply follow directions.) Then go on to the following action adapted specifically for men (male natural-actions are identified as "G" for Gentleman).

G-1 STANDING QUICK ENERGIZER

1. Stand erect in correct Boutelle alignment (Chapter III) . . . feet set comfortably a few inches apart . . . think IN, think UP . . . stand TALL, relaxed, not stiffly nor slumping or sagging . . . arms at sides naturally . . .

1

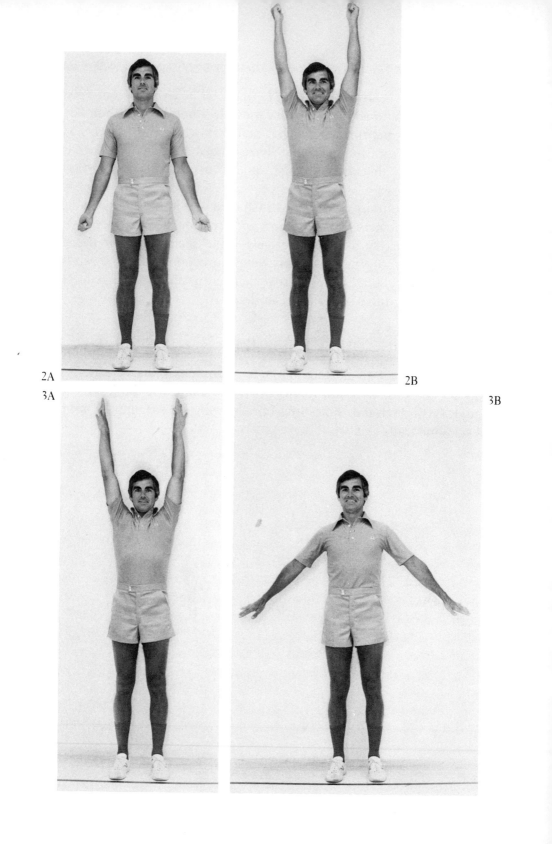

2A

2B

3A

3B

2a: *Inhale deeply* through your nose . . . and make tight fists (adds toning for your larger male arm and shoulder girdle muscles) . . . 2b: as you raise your straight arms slowly at your sides in an arc to high above your shoulders, each straight arm aligned with its respective shoulder cap, completing a circle above your head . . . feel your diaphragm lift as you fill up your lungs with oxygen, helping to lift your arms buoyantly . . .

3a: Now *exhale* forcefully through your mouth (blow like a whale!), blowing out carbon dioxide waste fully . . . as you release your fists, facing your palms away from your sides, stretching and spreading your fingers wide . . . 3b: and return your straight arms slowly at your sides to starting position.

Repeat the total action slowly *five times*—enjoy the smooth movements and energizing boost you get all over. Don't rush these actions—the basis of Boutelle conditioning is how smoothly and correctly, not how "fast" or how "hard" you move, to benefit you most. You *run smooth* always, never any potentially harmful forcing, jerking, or overstraining, always *playing safe*.

STARTING PROGRAM

It's essential to get your doctor's approval before undertaking this or any other conditioning program (show your physician this book). Observe all the points made in previous chapters—if you feel trembly, exhausted or strained at any point, STOP and rest.

As in my men's classes, you begin in a *straight-backed chair*, and start each session with this basic natural-action similar to the G-1 Quick Energizer.

G-2   OVER-SHOULDER STRETCH

1. Sit in correct alignment on your "sitting bones," feet a few inches apart . . . your back not touching the back of the chair. Flex your elbows and pull your lower arms up to wrap your spread fingers around your shoulder cap muscles (deltoids), each hand on its corresponding shoulder cap. *Exhale* (blow!) to force out carbon dioxide waste . . .

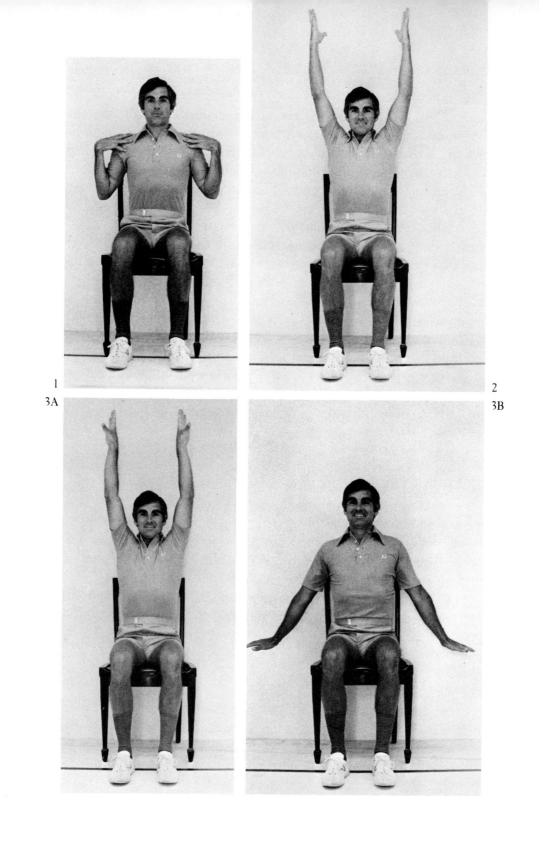

1

2

3A

3B

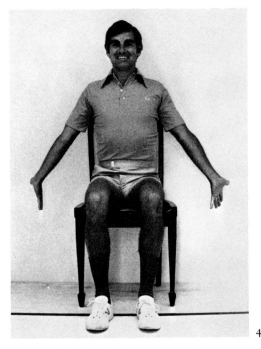

4

2. *Inhale deeply* as you raise your arms high over your shoulder caps, palms facing each other and fingers spread . . .

3a: *Exhale* forcefully as you rotate your stretched arms so palms face away from body, and—3b: slowly lower your arms until hands are at hip height, pushing down hard . . .

4. *Inhale*, rotating your straight arms so palms face up, and pulling arms up and overhead in a wide arc at sides . . .

5. *Exhale* as you flex your elbows and return arms and hands to the starting position, hands on shoulder caps.

Note: Throughout this natural-action, keep your head positioned so that your ears are dividing your shoulders . . . your neck zipped up . . . your focus straight ahead. You should not be able to see your arms as you perform this natural-action.

G-3 TRAPEZIUS TIGHTENER

This excellent natural-action reaches all the fibers of the large outer-layer *trapezius* upper back and shoulder muscle, a primary support for the male back particularly, and involved in raising the shoulders. Most of a man's usual actions in lifting the shoulders

1   2A   2B

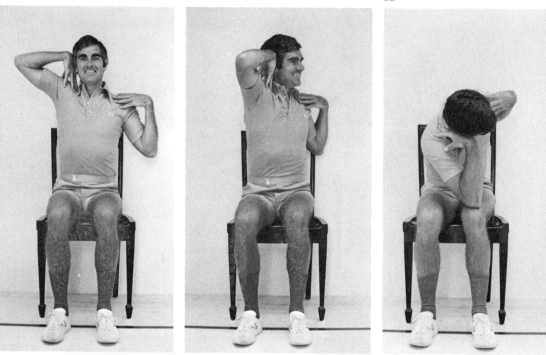

reach only the *upper* fibers of this massive muscle. Therefore the Trapezius Tightener effect is vital to your top fitness. As in every Boutelle natural-action, *run smooth* with every move, don't force or overstrain. Start in same position as G-2. *Exhale* forcefully . . .

1. *Inhale deeply* as you raise your *right* flexed arm as high as possible without straining, preferably until the back of your hand touches your ear (keeping your head and neck straight) . . . making sure that your right elbow remains in alignment with the side of the body, not thrusting forward or backward . . .

2a: *Exhale* as you twist your entire trunk slowly to face *left* . . .

2b—and bend to left carefully to bring your right elbow in contact with your left knee cap . . . do it smoothly, not forcing (feels good!) . . .

3. *Inhale* as you return slowly to position 2a . . .

4. *Exhale* as you return your flexed right arm to your side, hand back on shoulder cap, so you are in starting position again.

Now repeat entire action, but beginning with the *left* arm this time. Alternate right and left arm actions *ten times total* (five times with each arm). Your movements will become smoother and easier each day, and you will enjoy the flowing rhythm and exceptional benefits.

G-4 MALE PENDULUM SWING

Begin this male variation of the B-12 Pendulum Swing (Chapter VIII), seated in a chair, in aligned position, arms at your sides . . . hands relaxed toward the floor. (The female tailor-sit position on the floor is more natural for women because of the more flexible female pelvis.)

1. *Inhale deeply* as you flex your right wrist and rotate entire *right* arm clockwise so palm faces up . . . and swing your right arm, elbow locked, straight up in side arc to directly over right shoulder joint, as right palm (wrist flexed) exerts force in lifting-pushing action . . .

2. *Exhale* as you bend to the left, keeping your straight right arm in position over your right shoulder . . . and as you bend your body

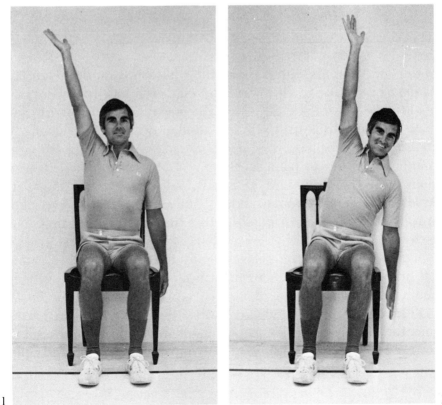

1   2

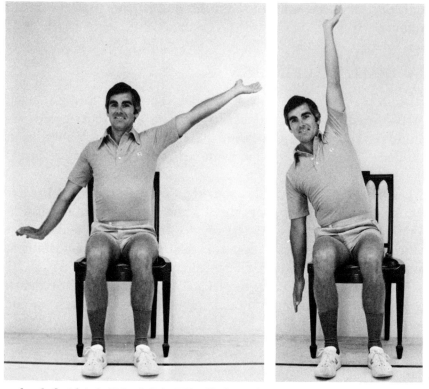

3   4

to the left (think IN, think UP all the while), fingertips of your left
hand will naturally reach toward and may even touch the floor . . .

3. *Inhale* as you stretch your right fingers, unflexing wrist, and
draw right arm back to straight-up position over right shoulder . . .
and *at same time* flex your *left* wrist and rotate entire *left* arm
counter-clockwise so palm faces up . . . and swing your left arm,
elbow locked, in its upward arc at side to directly over left shoulder.
As left arm ascends strongly and smoothly upward, lower your right
arm in side arc, back of hand leading the way, as you bring your
body up.

4. *Exhale* as right hand relaxes toward the floor naturally . . . and
left arm completes its pendulum swing over *right* shoulder as body
bends to the right . . .

Keep up the slow pendulum swing, the natural-action flowing
smoothly from side to side as you maintain your head and neck in
relaxed but stationary position as body moves (if you feel neck tight-
ness at any point, it's a signal of incorrect head movement, so check

yourself). Complete entire pendulum swings *five times* at first in continuous smooth, slow rhythm, gradually increasing day by day at your own comfortable pace to *ten times total*.

G-5   MAN'S GENTLE NECK STRETCH

Follow directions for A-7 (Chapter VII), except that you do this fine, relaxed natural-action seated in a straight chair with your arms comfortably at your sides.

G-6   MALE ROWING ACTION

Follow directions for A-8 (Chapter VII), but perform the rowing actions with your arms while seated in a straight chair. Be sure to keep your feet a few inches apart in correct alignment, feet flat on the floor and not shifting at all. You will enjoy the superb conditioning effect all over your body as you row-row-row.

G-7   MALE VARIATION OF THE WAVE

Follow directions for A-9 (Chapter VII), as you do this smooth-flowing action seated in straight chair, keeping your feet set firmly on the floor throughout. You will be flexing and extending the muscles supporting your spinal cord, and firming your midriff very effectively.

G-8   MAN'S ANKLE ACTIVATOR

This essential natural-action strengthens abdominal and lower back muscles as well as leg, ankle, and foot muscles. Concentrate on keeping your shoulders aligned correctly, pectoral pins firmly in place throughout (reread Chapter III). As you gain momentum in performing this action, concentrate on "whistling" air out in repeated short breaths—*whistle as you blow out each time*, improving your total conditioning.

   1: Sit in alignment in your chair . . . straighten legs to lock knee joints, lifting your legs straight forward and up as high as possible (don't force, you will attain improved straight-leg extension day after

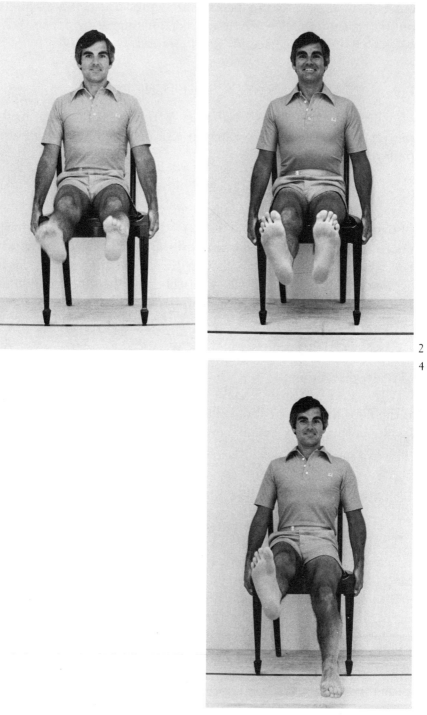

1

2

4

day) . . . be sure your legs stay in alignment a few inches apart, as always. Grasp chair seat with a hand on each side . . . point toes forward . . . keep elbows against sides of body throughout.

2. *Inhale* as you flex your ankle joints so toes turn up as far as possible . . .

3. *Exhale* as you extend ankle joints slowly and push toes forward to starting position. Repeat this 1-2 action with both feet simultaneously *ten times* . . . then alternate right foot and left foot actions in slow rhythm for another *ten times total*.

4. Now on to the second stage of the Activator—in same starting position, straight legs up: *Inhale* as you flex your *right* ankle . . . and reach for the floor with ball of your *left* foot at the same time, keeping both legs straight, knees locked . . .

5. *Exhale* as you lift and flex your *left* ankle . . . while reaching for the floor with ball of your *right* foot.

Repeat right-left up-down alternating actions in slow, smooth rhythm *ten times*.

PERFORM BASIC EIGHT DAILY

The preceding Basic Eight natural-actions for men provide a most effective and pleasurable session of under ten minutes. They require very little space, and no other equipment than the chair and you. Done faithfully day after day, these smooth, all-over natural-actions will help keep practically any man, including the fervent "weekend athlete," in top condition for work, recreation, sports. Without basic, all-over conditioning, you are far more prone to exhaustion, accidents, and injuries.

YOUR CONTINUING PROGRAM

After two weeks of the Basic Eight, you are ready for additional conditioning through the "A" Alpha program, done on the floor.

You have probably cut the time of each daily session as your muscular condition and performance have improved. Add a few more Alpha natural-actions within the ten minutes or more you can allot daily, or perhaps in a second session at another time each day. Proceed at your own pace and convenience, as follows (refer to Chapter VII):

For the third and fourth weeks, add A-1, A-2, A-3.

After two more weeks, add A-4, A-5, A-6.

Two weeks later, add A-10, A-11, A-12 (in doing this last natural-action, your arms may reach forward *beyond* the ankle joint, keeping heel of front foot always on the floor; the larger male arm and shoulder formations account for this change).

When you have completely mastered the combination "A" Alpha program, you can proceed to the male variation of the "B" Best Program (refer to Chapter VIII)—eliminating B-10, B-11, and B-12. As a general rule, the long-sit and stride-sit natural-actions described in "A" and "B" programs are to be avoided by men (with any exceptions noted), due to the male tighter pelvic structure and longer legs which make those positions naturally difficult for you.

I must emphasize again that if you feel strained at any time in performing any natural-action, STOP and rest. Never force yourself, never overstrain—your *safety* and comfort are paramount in Boutelle conditioning. You are improving your personal present and lifetime fitness, not competing with anyone. Easy does it, as your flexibility, coordination, and stamina will be improved smoothly, naturally, and enjoyably day after day, week after week.

You are on your way to your top lifetime fitness—to look, feel, and function better in everything you do from now on.

XIV
Checklist: Boutelle Lifetime Fitness Basics

• *All-over, inside-out neuromuscular conditioning* is the foundation of the carefully planned and proved Boutelle Method for Lifetime Fitness, unlike ordinary "calisthenics" or "exercises" which are often inadequate as well as faulty.

• *It's important to your health and fitness* that my program takes account of *inborn anatomical differences* between female and male, avoiding movements potentially harmful to the female body.

• *You feel improvement the first day* with no-strain natural-actions, and increasingly day by day as you develop "that beautiful Boutelle look" of perfect posture, balance, and alignment that others note and admire.

• *For all-day endurance,* neuromuscular conditioning builds improved, energizing *nerve-and-muscle* responses that replace old debilitating reactions causing tension and tiredness.

• *Muscles demand movement* or they deteriorate and waste away; your daily session activates all 632 muscles in your body to help you counteract fatigue and function smoothly and energetically.

• *You must continue natural-actions daily* because inactive muscles lose elasticity rapidly.

• *Boutelle natural-actions move deeply* into your respiratory and circulatory systems also, to promote your most healthful functioning.

• *Reserve a period of privacy* for your brief conditioning session every day; make others realize that this is not just something you "ought" to do, but that you *must* do to look, feel, and function at your very best

• *Always be alignment-aware* as you sit, stand, walk, in all daily actions as well as while doing Boutelle natural-actions—keep shoulders, hips, knees and ankles in correct alignment.

• *Remind yourself to think IN, think UP* for the proper posture necessary to look, feel, and function at your best all day, every day; remember to keep those "pectoral pins" IN.

• *Boutelle Rhythmic-Flow Breathing* is a must for top fitness: (1) inhale deeply through your nose . . . (2) exhale (BLOW LIKE A WHALE!) through your mouth; you must blow forcefully to *empty* your lungs of carbon dioxide waste before you can *fill* your lungs with life-supporting oxygen, so always breathe IN, BLOW OUT— out goes the bad air, in comes the fresh air.

• *Sit UP on your "sitting bones"* in chair, car, plane, everywhere; never slouch, sag, or slump into ungraceful, potentially harmful positions.

• *Stand TALL*—think IN, think UP, think of a magnet pulling your chest forward—for improved beauty, balance and endurance standing, walking, running.

• *Natural-actions trim off inches* by tightening and firming loose, sagging muscles which support your bones, to attain "sponge-cake firmness" and eliminate "layer-cake back" (rolls of flesh) and "marshmallow territory" (mushy swells in spots)—but to reduce overweight, you must diet.

• *You can trim "problem spots"* (flabby midsection, thighs, arms) only by doing special extra actions *after* attaining firm conditioning all over.

• *Advance always at your own pace*—don't compete, don't force—if it hurts, STOP at once.

• *What counts is HOW you move*, not how many times or how forcefully you move muscles and joints—so don't overexert, jerk, overstrain at any time.

• *You perform best in sports* only when your body is conditioned well all over for needed good coordination, balance, and stamina that support your sports moves and exertions properly.

• *You avoid many injuries* in everyday activities and sports when you have developed body balance and control through all-over neuromuscular fitness.

• *To help avoid painful back and other problems*, practice the Boutelle Bending-Down Action until it becomes part of your daily movements; do the same with elbows-in, push-pull, and overhead reach, lifting, carrying, sidestep, and other daily living actions.

• *Check the Medical Referral programs* for natural-actions for special problems, including lower back pain, arthritis, and others—and make doubly sure to check with your physician before proceeding.

• *Make it a prime rule* not to undertake this or any other movement program, including jogging and sports, without your doctor's examination and approval (show your physician this book); it is significant that a number of physicians and their wives are enrolled in and send patients to Boutelle Method classes.

• *S-M-I-L-E . . . fitness should be fun!*

• And remember, please, every day and always:
    Think IN!
    Think UP!

ACKNOWLEDGMENTS

Boutelle instructors shown in photographs:
Angela Curtis, Gail Dumas (Greenwich, Connecticut)
Gingie Greene (Shawnee Mission, Kansas)
Pamela Fleming (Mansfield, Ohio)
Nancy Gavrin (Scarsdale, New York)
Judy Williamson, Pat Stanley and her husband, Bill Stanley (Armonk, New York)

. . . and thanks to the many more Boutelle instructors not shown in photographs.

Photographs by Donna Gagliano
    (except for a few by Ned Roesler and Gretchen Tatge)
Drawings by Gerald J. Dumas

ABOUT THE AUTHORS

JANE BOUTELLE received her M.A. at Columbia, and then went into the field of teaching her specialty, movement education. This includes dance, body mechanics, and neuromuscular fitness. Her first class "Movement Exploration" was so successful at Marymount College, Tarrytown, New York, that she was asked to present a program for women of all ages at the White Plains, New York, YWCA. This course has in turn expanded in relatively few years to the enrollment of thousands of women annually in many classes in the area, and now it has spread to many communities in other parts of the country.

SAMM SINCLAIR BAKER, whom *The New York Times* has called "America's leading Self-Help author," is the coauthor of the five Dr. Irwin Stillman best-selling diet books: *The Doctor's Quick Weight Loss Diet, Dr. Stillman's Fourteen-day Shape-up Program, The Doctor's Quick Inches-Off Diet, The Doctor's Quick Weight Loss Diet Cookbook* and *The Doctor's Quick Teenage Diet*, as well as approximately twenty-five books, fiction and nonfiction. He has been published widely in national magazines and newspapers. He attended the University of Pennsylvania, Columbia University, New York University and the New School, and is a former president of an advertising agency. He has instructed courses in writing and advertising at New York University, Iona College, and the Mystery Writers of America.